Communicate

DAVID PAUL

book 1

Heinemann English Language Teaching
A division of Reed Educational and Professional Publishing Limited
Halley Court, Jordan Hill, Oxford OX2 8EJ

OXFORD MADRID FLORENCE ATHENS PRAGUE
SÃO PAULO MEXICO CITY CHICAGO
PORTSMOUTH (NH) TOKYO SINGAPORE
KUALA LUMPUR MELBOURNE AUCKLAND
JOHANNESBURG IBADAN GABORONE

Illustrated by:
Gary Andrews
Leendert Jan Vis
Peter Richardson
Lucy Maddison
Valerie Saunders

The author would like to thank everyone at
Heinemann for their hard work and support,
especially Valerie Gossage, Alix Harrower, Michael
Boyd, Vaughan Jones, Barton Armstrong, Richard
Kemp, and Mike Esplen. Yvonne de Henseler for her
enthusiasm and belief in the project.

Gary Andrews, Peter Richardson, Leendert Jan Vis,
Lucy Maddison, and Valerie Saunders for the great
artwork.

All the teachers and staff at David English House
who have contributed so many useful suggestions,
especially David Evans and Richard Walker.

Communicate Level 1 consists of:
Student's Book   435 26108 8 (Japanese edition)
Student's Book   435 26116 9 (International edition)
Workbook   435 26109 6
Teacher's Book   435 26110 X
Cassette   435 26111 8
CD   435 26117 7

Split editions:
Student's Book 1A 435 26119 3
Student's Book 1B 435 26120 7
Workbook 1A   435 26121 5
Workbook 1B   435 26122 3
Cassette 1A   435 26123 1
Cassette 1B   435 26124 X

Communicate Level 2 consists of:
Student's Book   435 26112 6
Workbook   435 26113 4
Teacher's Book   435 26114 2
Cassette   435 26115 0
CD   435 26118 5

Printed and bound in Spain by Cayfosa

96 97 98 99 10 9 8 7 6 5 4 3

Language Syllabus

One way of teaching a unit

There is no "right" way to use *Communicate*. Every teacher has a different style and every learning situation has its own unique requirements. The following way of teaching each section of a unit provides suggestions for teachers using the course for the first time. The aim is not to be prescriptive, but to suggest methods which can be successfully adapted to individual teaching styles and students' needs.

Lead-in

Aims: the introduction of new words and structures; the presentation of these new words and structures in short dialogues where they are linked with language the students already know.

Go through the following sequence with each dialogue/paragraph:

 1. Warm-up activity
Use one or more of the warm-up activities from pages 6 and 7 of this book (see the Teacher's Book for more specific suggestions). Warm-ups help "create a need" for the target words and structures, and enable the students to feel they are discovering this new language for themselves. Put the students in situations where they either need the target words and structures to express themselves, or where they need to guess the meaning of these structures. The students can then continue this activity among themselves (either as a group or in pairs).

 2. Listening (option)
Before playing the cassette or reading to the students, ask them one or two questions to focus on while listening. After finishing the dialogue/paragraph, ask the students for the answers to your questions. Either play the cassette or read again and follow up with comprehension/personalization questions, or go straight to the reading stage. If there is a comprehension stage, either you can ask questions or the students can ask each other the questions in the workbook.

 3. Reading
The students take roles or read in turn. Follow this up with comprehension/personalization questions. Either you can ask questions or the students can ask each other the questions in the workbook. These questions sometimes lead into a pairwork activity (see the Teacher's Book for ideas).

Word building

Aim: to practice vocabulary and expressions the students are likely to need when using the target language.

 Personalization
The students make individual sentences which include the words or expressions in this section. These sentences should be about themselves, their family, their city, their country, or something else they can genuinely relate to. Alternatively, the students could mime or make facial expressions to illustrate the differences between the words or expressions (e.g. to distinguish great, fine, not bad, and terrible in Unit 1).

Controlled practice

Aim: the consolidation of one of the new structures through the controlled use of picture prompts.

 Making sentences
The students look at the first picture and read what is written below it. Then, either individually or as a class, they try to make similar sentences, or questions and answers, about the other pictures.

Follow-up practice

Aim: to use a humorous dialogue as a model for either a role-play or self expression. This section provides the link between the previous three sections where the teacher is more in evidence, and the *Communication Activities* where the teacher takes a back seat.

 1. Warm-up activity
Use one or more of the warm-up activities from pages 6 and 7 of this book (see the Teacher's Book for more specific suggestions). The students can then continue this activity among themselves.

 2. Listening (option)
Before playing the cassette or reading to the students, ask them one or two questions to focus on while listening. After finishing the dialogue/paragraph, ask the students for the answers to your questions.

3. Reading
The students take roles or read in turn.

4. Pair practice
The students do the pairwork activity which is explained (for the teacher) at the bottom of the page. If necessary, help one pair demonstrate what to do in front of the class. Ideally, the students should do an imaginative role-play, but with some classes it may be best not to try this too soon. The extent to which you should be involved will also vary from class to class, but the more you can step back the better, so that the students are better prepared for the *Communication Activities*.

Communication Activities

Aim: to encourage the students to use the new words and structures in activities where they are completely relaxed and having a lot of fun. The first two activities in this section can be done without special equipment; the third activity requires photocopiable material from the Teacher's Book.

1. Setting up the activity
The students look at the picture of one of the activities and try to guess what to do. Help when necessary. If you are unsure how to do the activity, refer to the Teacher's Book for instructions. If the students come up with different ways of doing the activity, don't change what they are doing unless the language targets are not being practiced enough.

2. Total involvement
The students will need the new words and structures to express themselves, and the more involved they are in the activity the more spontaneously they will use this language. Pay close attention to what the students are doing, be available to answer their questions, and gently correct when necessary. Try not to interrupt the flow of the activity or reduce their involvement.

Consolidation Exercises

Aim: to consolidate the new words and structures through personalized sentences. These exercises can either be done orally or in writing.

1. Oral practice
The students can either do all the exercises orally, or just some, in preparation for writing.

2. Writing (option)
If the students are going to write their answers, have them practice orally first, so that all of them clearly understand what to do. They can then write their answers either at home or in class.

The Workbook

The first part of each unit in the workbook has comprehension/personalization questions which can be used for checking reading or listening comprehension. These questions can be used by the students in class (by themselves or in pairs) or at home. The second part of each unit contains puzzles. The aim of these puzzles is to increase the students' motivation and involvement, and to deepen their understanding of the usage of the new words and structures.

The Cassette

Contains all the dialogues/paragraphs in the *Lead-in* and *Follow-up* sections. These can either be used by the teacher in class, or by the student at home in combination with the workbook.

The Teacher's Book

Contains a step-by-step guide on how to teach each unit and provides the photocopiable material necessary for the third activity in each *Communication Activities* section.

Warm-up activities – ten ideas

Many approaches to teaching English start with a clear presentation or explanation by the teacher. In these approaches, dialogues or grammatical rules are generally used as models to substitute into. Self-motivated students are often glad to be taught in this way, probably because the initial clarity gives them a clear sense of direction (though this is not the only way of achieving this).

However, with less motivated students, these teacher-initiated approaches tend to encourage passive learning. Students who are taught like this may gain superficial knowledge, but are unlikely to produce much English spontaneously and communicatively.

In *Communicate*, the aim is to start with mystery, not clarity. When introducing new language targets, our main role as the teacher is to present the students with puzzles to solve. These puzzles are fun, pitched at the right level, and require the target language in order to be solved. The students' interest in solving the puzzles motivates them to search for the new language targets.

We never "teach". We create situations where the students are "learning" for themselves.

To do this effectively, it is crucial to select the right warm-up activity. When making this selection, the key question to ask ourselves is "Will this activity help the students feel they are learning what they want to learn, or will they simply feel they are learning what we want to teach?".

In the *Communicate Teacher's Book* specific warm-up activities are suggested for each of the language targets in the course. However, the activity chosen will vary a great deal depending on the class, so it is important to have a general overview of the options available. The ten types of activities outlined on these two pages are not comprehensive, but they should provide a quick reference and help you design your own alternative warm-up activities. Try these ones out! You'll be amazed at how popular and effective they are.

Note: The examples on this page show how one language target can be approached in a number of different ways.

Focused approach

Ask leading questions.
e.g. Target: **Have to**
T: *What time do you usually get up on Sunday?*
S: *Nine o'clock.*
T: *What time do you usually get up on Tuesday?*
S: *Six-thirty.*
T: *Six-thirty. Why not nine o'clock?*
S: *I ... (searching for how to say I have to go to school/ work.)*
If one student answers using "have to", the others can try and guess what "have to" means from this student's answer. If not, help one of the students use the pattern when he/she is trying to express him/herself. The students then ask each other similar questions, either in pairs or around the class.

Questioning

Ask the students questions which include the new language.
e.g. Target: **Have to**
T: *What do you have to do in the morning?*
S1: *Huh!*
T: *What do you have to do every day?*
S2: *I ...*
If none of the students guess how to answer, encourage them to ask you the questions and guess what "have to" means from your answers. The students then ask and answer similar questions, in pairs or around the class.

Disguised approach

Lead a simple, casual conversation towards a situation where the students need the target language to express themselves.
e.g. Target: **Have to**
Begin by talking about how nice the weather is, and suggest doing things which some students probably can't do because of other plans.
Say things like:
    Let's go to the beach tomorrow morning.
or *Let's go to a movie on Wednesday morning.*
The aim is to generate feelings like *I'm sorry I have to go to school*. If none of the students use "have to", help one of them use this pattern when he/she is trying to express him/herself. The students then make and accept/refuse similar suggestions, either in pairs or around the class.

Using the target in context

Make statements which include the target language and encourage the students to guess what you mean.
e.g. Target: **Have to**
T: *Oh no! I have to teach you again!*
    I have to get up at six o'clock in the morning!
    I have to come to school!
    I want to have breakfast, but I have to teach you!
Groan whenever you say "have to" and use a lot of humor. The students then talk about the things they have to do every day, either in pairs, in groups, or as a class.

Mime and pictures

The students make guesses about pictures or somebody miming.

e.g. Target: **Present continuous**

Mime some actions badly. The students try to guess what you are doing, saying things like *Are you swimming?* (if the students say things like *swim?*, help them use the tense correctly). Alternatively, half draw or gradually draw a picture of a person performing an action. The students can guess things like what a person is doing, is going to do, or did yesterday. The students then mime or draw pictures in front of the class, in groups, or in pairs.

Quizzes

Use the target language in a quiz and see if the students can guess how to answer the questions.

e.g. Target: **Occupations**

T : *He gets up at six-thirty every day.*
He wears a school uniform.
What does he do?

T: *She works in a hospital.*
She helps sick people.
What does she do?

If the students can't guess, give them two or three answers to choose from. They then try to think up similar quiz questions, and do the activity as a class or in pairs.

Word puzzles

Build-up the students' curiosity with a word puzzle.

e.g. Target: **All of us, most of us,**
                 some of us, none of us

Write the following on the board:

noses
study hard
don't do homework
gorillas

See if the students can solve the puzzle. If it is too difficult, ask questions like *How many of you are gorillas?* The class may decide that none of them do their homework or that some of them are gorillas, but that just adds to the fun.

The students then make their own sentences about the class, their family, their club, etc. using the four sentences *All of us..., Most of us ..., Some of us ..., None of us ...*

Brainstorming

The students say whatever they like about a subject.

e.g. Target: **Past simple**

Ask questions like,
        Who was Napoleon?
or   *Who was George Washington?*

Help the students use the past tense to tell you what they know about these people. Encourage the students not to worry about making mistakes. Help a little less each time you introduce a new historical figure. If it's not too difficult, the students can then try the activity among themselves, either as a class, in groups or in pairs.

Games

All the warm-up activities here are games, but there are some activities which are games in the more conventional meaning of the word.

e.g. Target: **possessives ('s)**

Ask one or more students to leave the room. While they are outside, get some or all of the other students to place one thing of theirs in a central place. When the students come back they have to guess who each thing belongs to. The first time, pick up one of the things and gesture to various students to hint who it might belong to. When the students who left the room are trying to say things like *I think it's Mario's*, help them say this.

Translation

Some teachers may find themselves in situations where they have to teach in the students' native language. In this case, the students can be given a series of sentences to translate into English (it is best if they write these sentences individually), starting with an easy sentence and ending with sentences which require the target language.

e.g. Target: **Past simple**

Write or say the following sentences in the students' language. The students translate them one by one.
        I play tennis every day.
        I can play tennis very well.
        Yesterday I played tennis for three hours.
(give the students the English word *yesterday*)
Let the students make guesses, and then give the correct answer (without saying why). Give them other similar sentences to translate. Continue until the students are beginning to recognize how the past simple is formed.

Lead-in

It's nice to meet you

Paula: Hello. I'm Paula.
I'm from Brazil.

Sachiko: It's nice to meet you.
I'm Sachiko. I'm from Japan.
This is Kim Jin Woo.
He's from Korea.

Paula: It's nice to meet you.

Kim: It's nice to meet you, too.

Paula: This is Marc.

Sachiko: Hi! How are you?

Marc: Pretty good thanks.

Sachiko: Are you French?

Marc: Yes, I am.

Sachiko: Where do you live?

Marc: Bordeaux. It's in the west of France.

Word building

Great!
Fantastic!

Fine.
Pretty good.

Not bad.
OK.

Not so good.
Terrible!

People and places

1

He lives in San Francisco.
It's in the west of the U.S.A.

2

_____ Rio Grande.
south

3

_____ Shanghai.
east

4

_____ Sapporo.
north

5

_____ Mexico City.
center

6

_____ Geneva.

Could you repeat that please?

ALIENS

GATES 21-30

Officer:	What's your name?
Alien:	Atchoo!
Officer:	How do you spell Atchoo?
Alien:	umm ... A-T-C-H-O-O
Officer:	Where are you from?
Alien:	I'm from Planet A-A-Atchoo!
Officer:	Sorry, could you repeat that please?
Alien:	I'm from Planet A-A-Atchoo!
Officer:	Thank you.

Pair practice

Student A: an immigration officer   Student B: him/herself, an alien, or a famous person
Student A asks the questions in the dialogue and other similar questions which he/she knows or can
guess how to say. Student B either gives true answers or plays the role of an alien or a famous person.

Communication Activities 1

A. Crossword

B. Newspaper reporters

C. Around the World

1 Consolidation Exercises

1 Where are they from?

a. Amadou's from Senegal,

in the _____ of Africa.

He lives in Dakar.

b. _____

_____

_____

_____

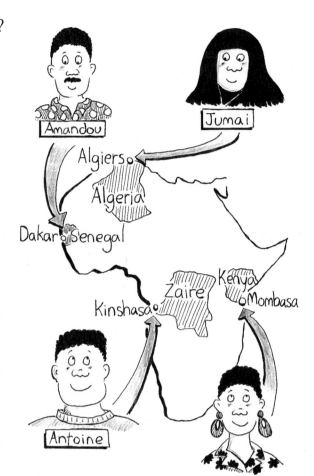

c. _____

_____

_____

_____

d. _____

_____

_____

_____

2 Is ... from ...?

a.

A: Is Lena from Italy?

B: No, she isn't.

A: Where's _____ ?

B: She's _____

b.

A: Is Carlos from Peru?

B: _____

A: _____ ?

B: _____

Questionnaire

What's your first name?

_____

What's your family name?

_____

Where are you from?

_____

What's your address?

_____

What's your telephone number?

_____

I don't like big cities

Manuel:	Do you live in Seoul?
Kim:	No, I live on Cheju Island.
Manuel:	Do you like it?
Kim:	Yes, very much.
	It's very quiet.
	I don't like big cities.
	They're so noisy and dirty.
Kim:	How about you, Manuel?
	Do you like the countryside
	or big cities?
Manuel:	Well, I live in Mexico City.
	It's very big and noisy,
	but I love it!
Kim:	Why?
Manuel:	I think the countryside's boring.

big (large)/little (small)   beautiful/ugly   exciting/boring

Adjectives

1

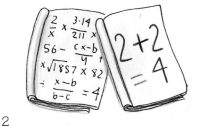
2

3

It's long./It's short.

4

5

6

easy   dirty   cheap   ~~long~~   noisy   clean   dangerous
quiet   safe   ~~short~~   difficult   expensive

What's your favorite sport?

Reporter:	What kind of TV shows do you like?
Caveman:	Movies and sports programs.
Reporter:	What kind of movies do you like?
Caveman:	Science fiction.
Reporter:	And what's your favorite sport?
Caveman:	Grand-prix racing.
Reporter:	Really?
Caveman:	Yes, it's very exciting! ... but, it's a little difficult.

Pair practice

Student A: the reporter   Student B: him/herself or a famous person
Student A asks the questions in the dialogue and other similar questions which he/she knows or can guess how to say. Student B gives true answers or plays the role of a famous person.

A. Starting letter

B. Chase the ace

C. Opinion poll

2 Consolidation Exercises

1 Like

Do you like Italian food or Chinese food?

I like _____

Do you like summer or winter?

_____

Do you like the city or the countryside?

_____

Do you like houses or apartments?

_____

2 Favorite

a. What's your favorite color?

My favorite _____

b. What's your favorite sports team?

_____

c. What's your favorite sport?

_____

d. Who's your favorite singer?

_____

3 Adjectives

a. It's expensive. _____

b. _____

c. _____

d. _____

Questionnaire

Where do you live?

_____

Do you like it?

_____

Why?

_____

What kind of movies do you like?

_____

Why?

_____

Who's your favorite movie star?

_____

Why?

_____

4 What do you think of ...?

a. big cities   I think they are _____

b. the countryside   _____

c. your house (or apartment)   _____

d. your teacher   _____

e. your job (or school)   _____

Locations

telephoning ♦ 1

Lead-in

Where are you now?

Sachiko: Hello.

Marc: Hello, Sachiko.
This is Marc.

Sachiko: Hi, Marc!
How are you?

Marc: Pretty good.

Sachiko: Where are you now?

Marc: At a coffee shop near
the beach.

Marc: Are you busy tonight?

Sachiko: Not really.

Marc: Do you like jazz?

Sachiko: Yes, I love it.

Marc: Let's go to the jazz club on
Main Street.

Sachiko: That's a great idea!

Marc: Let's meet in the bar next
to the club at seven o'clock.

Sachiko: All right!

Marc: See you at seven.

Sachiko: Goodbye.

Word building

| in | on | under | next to (beside) | near |

Downtown

1

The bank's next to the bookstore.

2

The bowling alley's _____

3

The coffee shop's _____

4

The gym's _____

5

The library's _____

6

The disco's _____

Where are my teeth?

Dracula:	Where are my socks?
Mrs. Dracula:	They're under the newspaper on the table.
Dracula:	Where's my cape?
Mrs. Dracula:	It's in the closet near the door.
Dracula:	... And where are my teeth?
Mrs. Dracula:	They're in the glass on the shelf.

Pair practice

Student A: asks where things are in the room, or where places are in the neighborhood, the country, etc.
Student B: if A asks about things in the room, B closes his/her eyes and tries to answer. If A asks about places in the city, country, etc., B tries to give the exact location. B scores one point for each correct answer.

18

A. Where are they in your house?

B. Neighborhoods

C. Hiding in a picture

3 Consolidation Exercises

1 Where's the ...?

a. Where's the library?

It's _____

b. Where's the coffee shop?

_____

c. Where's the bookstore?

_____

d. Where's the post office?

_____

e. Where's the department store?

_____

f. Where's the ice-cream parlor?

_____

2 On the telephone

Sachiko: Hello.

You: Hello, Sachiko. _____

This is _____

Sachiko: Hi!

How are you?

You: _____

Sachiko: Where are you now?

You: _____

_____

You: Are you busy tonight?

Sachiko: Not really.

You: Let's _____

Sachiko: OK

You: Let's meet _____

_____

_____

Sachiko: All right.

See you at _____

You: _____

3 Let's meet ...

Let's meet _____

bookstore _____

_____

at _____

Questionnaire

Where are you from?

_____

Where do you live?

_____

Where's your house (or apartment)?

_____

Where's your English class?

_____

Directions

imperatives

Lead-in

How do I get to the Art Park?

Lee: Excuse me.

Manuel: Yes?

Lee: How do I get to the Art Park?

Manuel: Go straight down this street.
Take the second left.
Then, take the first right.
It's on the left.

Carmen: Manuel! That's not the Art Park! That's the parking lot!

Carmen: I'm sorry. His English is terrible.

Lee: No problem.

Carmen: Go straight down this street.
Go past the post office.
Go over the bridge,
... and it's in front of you.

Lee: Thank you very much.

Carmen: You're welcome.

Word building

on the left

on the right

in front of
the department store

behind
the station

across from
(opposite)
the bank

Directions

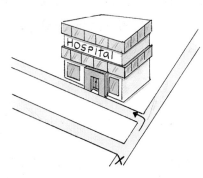

1

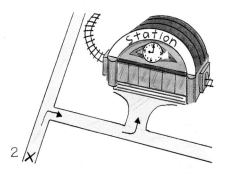

2

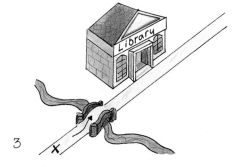

3

Take the second left.
The hospital's on the right.

_____

_____

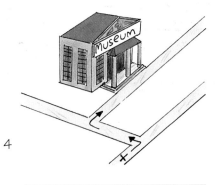

4

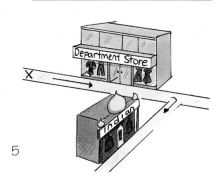

5

6

_____

_____

_____

Yes, boss

Scarface:	Listen Luigi! Go out of this building and turn left.
Luigi:	Yes, boss.
Scarface:	Take the second right.
Luigi:	Yes, boss.
Scarface:	The garage is on the left. Go into the garage and put this package in the police car.
Luigi:	Yes, boss. Is it a Christmas present, boss?
Scarface:	No, Luigi. It's a bomb. So be careful! Walk! Don't run! And don't drop it!
Luigi:	Yes, boss.

Pair practice

Student A gives Student B directions to a place nearby (e.g. a store or an office) and tells him/her to do something
when he/she gets there (e.g. "Go into the donut shop and get a coconut donut and a strawberry milkshake.").

A. Directions

B. Bulls-eye

C. Maps of New York and London

4 Consolidation Exercises

1 Where's the ...?   across from/behind/in front of

a. Where's the bank?

   It's _____

b. Where's the art gallery?

   _____

c. Where's the bus stop?

   _____

d. Where's the hotel?

   _____

2 Excuse me

a. Excuse me. How do I get to the bus stop?

   Take the first left. _____

   It's in front of the station. _____

b. Excuse me. How do I get to the art gallery?

   _____

   _____

c. Excuse me. How do I get to the bank?

   _____

d. Excuse me. How do I get to the hotel?

   _____

3 Go ...

a.   Go past a/the hotel. _____

b.   _____

c.   _____

Questionnaire

Excuse me. How do I get to your home?

_____

_____

_____

_____

Excuse me. How do I get to the station?

_____

_____

_____

_____

There is · there are 5

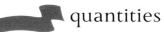

quantities

Lead-in

There are some trees on the left

Paula: Do you like my painting?

Lee: Well ... yes ... but, what is it?

Paula: It's a landscape.
Look! There's a hill in the middle.
And there are some trees
on the left and on the right.

Lee: I see. And is that a house
at the bottom on the right?

Paula: No, that's a cow!

Paula: Where are you from?

Lee: Shanghai.

Paula: I don't know China very well.
Tell me about Shanghai.

Lee: Well, it's a very large city. There are
a lot of old European buildings. And
there are some fantastic theaters,
concert halls, and art galleries!

Paula: How many people are there?

Lee: I think there are about twelve million.

Paula: Twelve million! That's big!

Word building

top

bottom

middle

above

below

In the office

1

There's a photocopier.

2

There are some filing cabinets.

3

There aren't any armchairs.

4

_____ calculators.

5

_____ fax.

6

_____ gorillas.

There are a lot of high mountains

Cow:	Where are you from?
Horse:	Spain.
Cow:	Are there any high mountains in Spain?
Horse:	Yes, there are a lot of high mountains.
Cow:	Are there any beautiful beaches?
Horse:	Yes, there are a lot of beautiful beaches.
Cow:	Are there a lot of handsome bulls?
Horse:	Uh ... There are a few, but they are very dangerous.

Pair practice

Student A: thinks of a country or area of his/her country which he/she knows something about.
Student B: asks Student A questions using the pattern "Are there ... in ...?"

A. Discovering a picture

B. Where am I from?

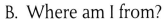

C. What are the differences?

5 Consolidation Exercises

1 Yes / No

Are there a lot of tall buildings in New York?
Yes, there are.

Are there any people on the moon?
_____

Is there a river near your house?
_____

Are there a lot of kangaroos in Tokyo?
_____

2 In the picture

a. There are some flowers at the bottom on
the left.

b. _____

c. _____

d. _____

3 Countries

There are some fantastic
festivals in Brazil.

_____

_____

Questionnaire

Your town/city
There _____

_____

_____

_____

Your country

_____

_____

_____

Have · want · would like

shopping ·1

Lead-in

I have a great car!

Marc: Let me drive you home.

Sachiko: No, don't worry. I'm all right.

Marc: I have a great car!

Sachiko: What kind is it?

Marc: It's a Ferrari.

Sachiko: A Ferrari! Wow!

Marc: Yes. It has power steering, tinted windows, a sunroof ... and it has a TV, and a fantastic sound system.

Sachiko: Um ... Marc ... Please drive me home.

Marc: Sure.

Lee: Do you have any brothers or sisters?

Paula: Yes, I have a little brother. He has purple hair! And he's crazy about rock music!

Lee: I don't have a brother. But, I have a little sister. She's crazy about motorcycles. She wants a Harley Davidson!

Word building

Carmen's crazy about (loves) surfing.

Michelle likes spaghetti.

Manuel doesn't like dogs.

Kim hates pop music.

29

want / would like

1

2

3

He wants a new briefcase.
He'd like a new briefcase.

_____

_____

4

5

6

_____

_____

Do you have any shirts?

Clerk:	May I help you?
Atchoo:	Yes. Do you have any shirts?
Clerk:	Sure. What color would you like?
Atchoo:	Green, please.
Clerk:	What size are you - large, medium, or small?
Atchoo:	I don't know. I think I'm a medium.
Clerk:	How about this one?
Atchoo:	Yes, it's very nice.
Clerk:	Would you like to try it on?
Atchoo:	Yes, please. ... Oh dear! It only has two sleeves!

Pair practice

Student A: a clerk in any kind of store   Student B: him/herself or a famous person
Student A asks similar questions to the ones in the dialogue and any other appropriate questions which he/she knows or can guess how to say. Student B imagines what he/she or a famous person would say.

Communication Activities 6

A. Go Fish

B. Vampire grid game

C. Shopping role-play

6 Consolidation Exercises

1 Yes, I do. / No, I don't.

Do you have a driver's license?

_____

Do you have any pets?

_____

Do you have a Rolls Royce?

_____

Do you have any compact discs?

_____

Do you have a personal computer?

_____

Do you have any children?

_____

2 Your family and friends

```
_____ Me _____
___ I'm crazy about _____
___ I like _____
___ I don't like _____
___ I hate _____
___ I have _____
___ I 'd like _____
```

```
___ My _____
___ 's crazy about _____
___ likes _____
___ doesn't like _____
___ hates _____
___ has _____
___ 'd like _____
```

```
___ 's crazy about _____
___ likes _____
___ doesn't like _____
___ hates _____
___ has _____
___ 'd like _____
```

3 At the store

Clerk: May I help you?

You: _____ ?

Clerk: Sure.
        What color would you like?

You: _____

Clerk: What size are you?

You: _____

Clerk: How about this one.

You: _____

Questionnaire

Do you have any brothers or sisters?

_____

_____

What kind of television do you have?

_____

What do you want?

1. _____

2. _____

3. _____

4. _____

Uncountable nouns

at a restaurant

Lead-in ## There isn't any food!

Manuel: Who's that?

Carmen: It's me. I'm hungry!

Manuel: At three o'clock in the morning!

Carmen: Yes, I'm starving!
But look at this!
There's a large can of beer!
There are ten bottles of tequila!
And there's some brandy, some
sake, some gin, some whiskey ...
But, there isn't any food!

Manuel: How much vodka is there?

Carmen: About five bottles!

Manuel: How many slices of lemon
are there?

Carmen: Just three or four.

Manuel: Let's make some cocktails.

Carmen: At three o'clock in the morning!

Manuel: I'm thirsty!

Word building

a little
butter

a lot of
money

a carton
of milk

a slice of
bread

a bowl
of soup

In the kitchen

There's a microwave.

_____ some pots.

_____ some bread.

_____ chairs.

_____ cooking oil.

Would you like some garlic bread?

Waiter:	What would you like?
Dracula:	I'd like some soup, a big steak, and some ice cream please.
Waiter:	What kind of soup would you like? Tomato or mushroom?
Dracula:	Tomato, please.
Waiter:	Would you like your steak rare, medium, or well-done?
Dracula:	Very rare, please.
Waiter:	And would you like some garlic bread?
Dracula:	Garlic! ... N-n-no, thank you.

Pair practice

Student A: a waiter   Student B: a customer ordering a meal
Students can use the above dialogue as a model, but imagine they are in various kinds of restaurants.

A. What's on the tray?

B. Prompts

C. Menus

7 Consolidation Exercises

1 On the breakfast table

a. There's a _____ vase.

b. There are some _____ saucers.

c. There's some _____ sugar.

d. There aren't any _____ bananas.

e. There isn't any _____ gasoline.

f. _____ cups.

g. _____ bread.

h. _____ coffee pot.

i. _____ fried eggs.

j. _____ wine.

2 How many?

a. How many snakes are there?

_____

b. How many spiders are there?

_____

c. How many vampires are there?

_____

3 How much?

a. How much milk is there?

There's one _____ carton.

b. How much pizza is there?

_____ slices.

c. How much water is there?

_____ glass.

d. How much rice is there?

_____ bowl.

e. How much coffee is there?

_____ cups.

f. How much money is there?

_____ a lot.

Questionnaire

In my kitchen

1. There _____

2. _____

3. _____

In my refrigerator

1. _____

2. _____

3. _____

In my pocket/bag

1. _____

2. _____

3. _____

Lead-in | David's apartment

David's apartment is on the third floor of an apartment building. It's small and messy. His books and clothes are all over the floor, and there are pictures of his favorite soccer teams all over the walls.

Paula's apartment is on the second floor. It has a bedroom, a living room, and a small studio. There's some beautiful antique furniture in her living room and there are a lot of very interesting paintings in her studio.

Sachiko and Michelle share an apartment on the first floor. Their apartment is modern and comfortable, and it has a large yard. There's a piano in their living room, and there's a swimming pool in their yard.

Word building

This is mine!
And this is yours!

That pizza's his!
And that drink's hers!

These are theirs!
Those are ours!

At Carmen's house

Whose painting is that?

Reporter: Wow! Whose painting is that?

Caveman: It's mine.

Reporter: And whose chair is this?

Caveman: It's Donald's.

Reporter: It's very big!

Caveman: Yes. Donald's big.

Reporter: Uh ... Who's Donald?

Caveman: He's my pet dinosaur.

Reporter: A dinosaur!
... D-d-does he like reporters?

Caveman: Yes, very much ...
... for breakfast.

Pair practice

Student A: is a reporter and asks questions about things in the room or in a picture, using the following framework:
A: Whose ... is this/that? B: It's X's. A: Who's X? B: He/she's ... If appropriate, A can ask more questions about X.

Communication Activities 8

A. Guess who

B. Bleep

C. Whose is it?

8 Consolidation Exercises

1 Whose?

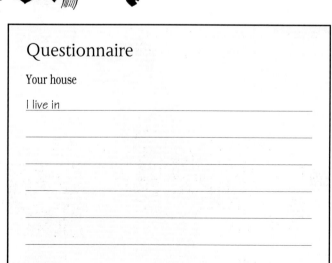

Yoko

a. Whose camera is it?

It's Yoko's.

Mike

b. Whose cassettes are they?

Jinsook

c. Whose guitar is it?

Mohammed

d. Whose videos are they?

Christina

e. Whose briefcase is it?

Colin

f. Whose bananas are they?

2 Family and friends

My grandfather's dog
is very dangerous.

_____ 's

_____ 's

3 Houses and apartments

My friend lives in _____

_____

_____

_____

My _____

4 Dracula

His teeth are long.

_____ big.

_____ short.

_____ dirty.

Questionnaire

Your house

I live in _____

Lead-in   ## I'm cooking dinner

Michelle: Hello.

David: Hello. This is David.
Could I speak to Sachiko,
please?

Michelle: Sure. Just a minute.

Sachiko: Hello.

David: Hi, Sachiko.
What are you doing?

Sachiko: I'm cooking dinner.

David: What's Michelle doing?

Sachiko: She's studying.
And Paula's here, too.
She's playing the piano.
Hey! Would you like to
have dinner with us?

David: I'd love to!

Sachiko: Great! But dinner's nearly
ready, so please hurry!

Word building

I'm sorry, she's out.

Just a minute. (Please hold on.)

Please call back later.

Sunday afternoon

1

She's playing volleyball.

2

They're _____

3

He's _____

4

He's _____

5

She's _____

6

They're _____

Maybe it's a Christmas present

Policeman:	Luigi is going out of the building.
H.Q.:	Is he turning left?
Policeman:	Yes, he is.
H.Q.:	Is he going to the airport?
Policeman:	No, I don't think so. Now, he's turning right. He's going into my garage!
H.Q.:	Your garage!
Policeman:	Yes ... and now he's putting a package in my car.
H.Q.:	Maybe it's a Christmas present.
Policeman:	In July! ... Now he's getting out of my car ... and he's slamming the door.

BANG

Pair practice

Student A: mimes or draws pictures of a sequence of actions (e.g. getting up, cooking dinner).
Student B: tries to guess what Student A is miming or drawing.

A. Telepathy

B. Name a time

C. Detectives

9 Consolidation Exercises

1 What are they doing?

a. What's she doing?

She's eating spaghetti.

b. _____

c. _____

d. _____

e. _____

2 I think ...

What's your teacher doing?

I think she/he's _____

What's your favorite singer doing?

_____

What's your best friend doing?

_____

What's your brother (or sister) doing?

_____

What's your favorite movie star doing?

_____

What's your father (or mother) doing?

_____

3 On the telephone

You:	Hello.
Sachiko:	Hello. This is Sachiko.
You:	_____?
Sachiko:	Pretty good. How are you?
You:	_____
Sachiko:	Are you busy today?
You:	_____
Sachiko:	What are you doing?
You:	_____
	_____?
Sachiko:	I'm watching television. What's your family doing?
You:	My _____
	My _____
	My _____
Sachiko:	OK. See you.
You:	_____

Questionnaire

Where do you live?

_____

Do you like big cities or small towns?

_____

Why? _____

What kind of TV shows do you like?

_____

What's your favorite color?

_____

Where are you now?

_____

What are you doing?

_____

44

Fashion  10

shopping ◆ 2

Lead-in Marc's wearing a leather jacket

David and his friends are playing soccer against a team of students. Manuel, Kim, and Michelle are playing for the students' team. David's team is wearing light blue shirts and dark blue shorts. The students' team is wearing red and white striped shirts and white shorts.

Paula, Sachiko, Marc, and Carmen are watching the game. Paula's wearing a light green blouse and white slacks. Sachiko's wearing a yellow blouse and a beige skirt. Marc's wearing a leather jacket and blue jeans, and Carmen's wearing a green dress.

Word building

It's out of fashion.   It's in fashion.   It looks good on him.   It doesn't look good on him.

45

Clothes

1   2   3

She's wearing _____

_____   _____

_____   _____

tight   striped   high heels   fashionable   sun hat   running shoes   loose
plain   jeans   shirt   blouse   sandals   swimsuit   skirt

Follow-up practice   Short skirts are in fashion

Julius: Do you have any red skirts?

Clerk: Yes. How about this one?

Julius: It's a little short.

Clerk: Yes, but short skirts are in fashion.
        Would you like to try it on?

Julius: Oh, all right.

Julius: It looks strange.

Clerk: No, you look great!

Julius: Really? Do you think so?
        How much is it?

Clerk: $1,000.

Julius: Is that cheap or expensive?

Clerk: Oh, very cheap!

Julius: And um ... Do I really look great?

Clerk: Sure. You look fantastic!

Pair practice

Student A: a clerk in any kind of store   Student B: him/herself or a famous person
The students start off by using the above dialogue as a model, substituting new language to fit the situation.

A. Fashion parade

B. Guess who

C. What are the differences?

10 Consolidation Exercises

1 What are they wearing?

She's wearing _____

_____

_____

_____

_____

_____

_____

_____

_____

_____

_____

_____

2 At a store

Clerk: May I help you?

You: _____

_____?

Clerk: What size are you?

You: _____

Clerk: How about this one?

You: _____

Clerk: Yes, but _____ are in fashion.

Would you like to try it on?

You: _____

_____?

Clerk: $500.

You: _____?

Clerk: Oh, very cheap!

You: _____?

Clerk: Sure. You look beautiful!

Questionnaire

What clothes are in fashion?

_____

_____

What clothes are out of fashion?

_____

_____

What clothes look good on you?

_____

_____

What clothes don't look good on you?

_____

_____

What are you wearing?

_____

_____

Lead-in ## I can't swim!

Marc: I can speak French, German, Italian, and a little English! And I can play a lot of sports, too. I can play baseball, basketball, tennis, badminton, and a lot of other sports.

Carmen: That's great!

Manuel: Can you swim?

Marc: Yes, I'm a very good swimmer! ... No! Help!

SPLASH!

Marc: Help! I can't swim!

Marc: Hello.

Sachiko: Hi, Marc! It's me, Sachiko. Let's go to a movie this afternoon!

Marc: I'm sorry, I can't.

Sachiko: Well, let's have dinner tonight!

Marc: No, I can't meet you tonight. Atchoo!!

Sachiko: Are you all right?

Marc: No, I feel terrible.

Sachiko: Oh dear!

Word building

Lee can play baseball.

Paula can play the guitar.

Manuel and Carmen can sail.

我會說國語

Kim can speak Chinese.

can

1

She can ski.

2

_____

3

_____

4

_____

5

_____

6

_____

Follow-up practice ## Can you play the Moonlight Sonata?

Pirates:	Jump!
Man:	I can't swim!
Pirates:	Jump!
Man:	Look … I can sew, I can iron, I can wash the dishes …
Pirates:	Jump!
Man:	… I can cook …
Pirate:	Jump!
Man:	… and … I can play the piano.
Captain:	Can you play the Moonlight Sonata?
Man:	Yes, I love Mozart.
Captain:	Mozart! It's not by Mozart! It's by Beethoven!
Pirates:	Jump!!

Pair practice

Student A: the pirate captain saying "Jump" or "OK. Don't Jump" to Student B
Student B: him/herself or a famous person on the plank of the pirate ship. He/she has to give good reasons for not having to jump, using the pattern "I can …".

A. Newspaper reporters

B. I can see ...

C. Survivors

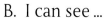

11 Consolidation Exercises

1 Yes, I can. / No, I can't.

Can you swim?

_____

Can you drive?

_____

Can you speak Chinese?

_____

Can you type?

_____

Can you play baseball?

_____

Can you play the guitar?

_____

2 Your family and friends

Me
I can _____
I can't _____

___ can _____
___ can't _____

___ can _____
___ can't _____

3 I'm sorry, I can't. / Yes, I'd love to!

Would you like to go to a concert tonight?

_____

Would you like to go to a party on Saturday?

_____

Would you like to go to the beach tomorrow?

_____

Would you like to go to Hawaii on Sunday?

_____

4 Jump!

Pirates: Jump!

You: I can't swim.

Pirates: Jump!

You: _____

Pirates: Jump!

You: _____

Pirates: Jump!

You: _____

Pirates: Jump!

You: _____

Pirates: OK. Don't jump!

You: Thank you.

Questionnaire

What sports can you play?

_____

_____

What musical instruments can you play?

_____

_____

What languages can you speak?

_____

_____

What can you see?

1. _____

2. _____

3. _____

Lead-in   What do you do?

David: What do you do, Lee?

Lee: I'm a doctor. How about you?

David: I'm an English teacher.
These are my students.

Lee: How about you, Sachiko?
What do you do?

Sachiko: I'm a stewardess.

Lee: Wow! Really?

David: Yes, she travels all over the world.

Lee: What does Michelle do?

David: She's an exchange student.

Lee: How long is she here?

David: About a year.
Kim's here for a year, too.
But, the other students are
only here for two or three months.

Lee: What does Michelle study?

David: Computer science.

Word building

She studies science.   **He studies** history.   **She studies** economics.   **They study** engineering.

Occupations

1

She's a lawyer.

2

He's a civil servant.

3 _____

4 _____

5 _____

6 _____

My husband works very hard

Mona: My husband works very hard.
He works at night and he works
on Sundays. But he wears a very
nice uniform!

Lisa: What does he do?

Mona: He's a policeman.

Lisa: My husband works hard, too.

Mona: Does he make a lot of money?

Lisa: Yes, he does.

Mona: Is he a doctor?

Lisa: No, he isn't.

Mona: Does he work in a bank?

Lisa: Uh … Yes, he does!

Pair practice

Student A: thinks of somebody he/she knows well.
Student B: asks Yes/No questions to try and find out the occupation of the person Student A is thinking about.

A. What's my job?

B. Last sentence

C. Concentration

12 Consolidation Exercises

1 What do they do?

a. _____   b. _____   c. _____

2 Yes, I do. / No, I don't.

Do you make a lot of money?   Do you wear a uniform?   Do you use a computer?

_____   _____   _____

Do you work in an office?   Do you work/study hard?   Do you have long vacations?

_____   _____   _____

3 What do they study?   math/art/science/history/engineering/medicine/English/economics

a. _____She studies_____   b. _____   c. _____   d. _____
_____science._____

e. _____   f. _____
_____   _____

g. _____   h. _____

Questionnaire

What do you do?

_____

Do you like it?

_____

Why?   .

_____

Your work/school

1. _I don't make a lot of money._____

2. _____

3. _____

4. _____

56

I always eat out

Sachiko: What time do you usually get up?

Marc: At about eleven o'clock.

Sachiko: Eleven o'clock!

Marc: Yes, I hate getting up early.

Sachiko: Do you have breakfast?

Marc: Yes, but I usually just have coffee and toast.

Sachiko: What do you have for lunch?

Marc: I often have spaghetti or pizza.

Sachiko: How about dinner?

Marc: I always eat out.
I often go to an Indian restaurant.

Sachiko: What do you do in the afternoon?

Marc: I sometimes go to the beach, and I sometimes go to a recording studio.

Sachiko: How about in the evening?
What do you do after dinner?

Marc: I usually practice with my band.
I never get home before midnight.

never   sometimes   often   usually   always

57

A superstar's day

1

She usually wakes up
at ten o'clock.

2

_____ has breakfast

3

_____ goes to sleep again

4

_____ gets up

5

_____ goes to a party

6

_____ goes to bed

Is he dangerous?

Caveman: Don't forget! He always has breakfast at seven-thirty.

Reporter: What time does he have lunch?

Caveman: He usually has lunch at twelve o'clock.

Reporter: What does he do in the afternoon?

Caveman: He sometimes goes to the park, and he sometimes goes to the gym.

Reporter: What does he do in the evening?

Caveman: He always watches TV. He never goes out.

Reporter: ... I-i-is he dangerous?

Caveman: Yes, he's sometimes dangerous before breakfast ... so, be careful!

Pair practice

The students look at pictures of people or animals (magazine pictures, photographs, this book, etc.).
Student A: asks questions about the person's/animal's daily routine.
Student B: answers the questions, possibly using the pattern "I think ...".

Communication Activities 13

A. Twenty questions

B. Famous people

C. Housework

13 Consolidation Exercises

1 always/usually/often/sometimes/never ... on Sunday

I _____ eat spaghetti.   I _____ have breakfast in bed.
I _____ cook dinner.   I _____ watch television.
I _____ play soccer.   I _____ go to bed after midnight.
I _____ go to the gym.   I _____ drink champagne.

2 Your family and friends

_____ Me
____ always _____
____ usually _____
____ often _____
____ sometimes _____
____ never _____

_____
____ always _____
____ usually _____
____ often _____
____ sometimes _____
____ never _____

_____
____ always _____
____ usually _____
____ often _____
____ sometimes _____
____ never _____

_____
____ always _____
____ usually _____
____ often _____
____ sometimes _____
____ never _____

Questionnaire

What time do you usually get up?   What do you usually do in the morning?

_____   _____

What do you usually do in the afternoon?   What do you usually do after dinner?

_____   _____

What do you usually have for breakfast?   What do you usually have for lunch?

_____   _____

What do you usually have for dinner?   What time do you usually go to bed?

_____   _____

Lead-in How do you get to work?

Manuel: How do you get to work?

Kim: I always go by car.
How about you?

Manuel: I sometimes ride my bike
and I sometimes walk.

Kim: How long does it take?

Manuel: By bike it takes ten minutes,
and on foot about half an hour.
How long does it take you?

Kim: An hour and a half!

Kim: What time do you get home?

Manuel: I sometimes have meetings
after work, but I always get
home before seven-thirty.

Kim: You're lucky! I work from eight-thirty
in the morning until about
ten o'clock at night.

Word building

Carmen goes to work by car.
(She drives to work.)

Lee goes to work by train.
(He takes a train to work.)

Michelle goes to school on foot.
(She walks to school.)

Going to work

1

She goes to work by bus.
She takes a bus to work.

2 _____

3 _____

4 _____

5 _____

6 _____

How do I get to the Central Bank?

Robber: Excuse me. How do I get to the Central Bank from here?

Policeman: Take a number 6 bus. The bus stop is in front of the supermarket.

Robber: How long does it take?

Policeman: About fifteen minutes. Get off in front of the station.

Robber: How far is it from the station to the bank?

Policeman: About 100 meters.

Robber: Thank you.

Pair practice

The students ask and answer how to get to local places starting from different places in their city/town.

62

A. Lifestyles

B. Where is it?

C. Schedules

14 Consolidation Exercises

1 How do they get to work/school?

a. She goes to work by bus.   b. _____   c. _____

She takes a bus to work.   _____   _____

2 How long does it take?

a. It takes about _____   b. _____   c. _____

_____   _____   _____

3 Excuse me ...

How do I get to the station?

Take a _____

_____

How do I get to the library?

_____

_____

4 How long do they work?

He usually works _____

_____ in the

morning _____

_____ at night.

_____

_____

_____

_____

Questionnaire

What do you do?

_____

How do you get to work/school?

_____

How long does it take?

_____

How far is it?

_____

What time do you usually get home?

_____

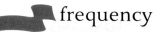

Lead-in ## How often do you go back to Korea?

Kim: Hi, Carmen!
Where's Manuel?

Carmen: I'm not sure.
I think he's playing tennis.
He usually plays tennis
on Friday afternoon.

Kim: And what are you doing here?

Carmen: I'm just looking.

Carmen: How about you?
What are you doing?

Kim: I'm buying a ticket to Egypt.

Carmen: That's great!
You need a vacation.

Kim: Yes, I know.
I only take a vacation once a year.
So, I'm really looking forward to it.

Carmen: How often do you go back to Korea?

Kim: About once every two months.
But, I always go on business.

Word building

S M T W T F S	S M T W T F S	S M T W T F S	S M T W T F S	S M T W T F S
1 2 3 4 5 6 7	1 2 3 4 5 6 7	1 2 3 4 5 6 7	1 2 3 4 5 6 7	1 2 3 4 5 6 7
8 9 10 11 12 13 14	8 9 10 11 12 13 14	8 9 10 11 12 13 14	8 9 10 11 12 13 14	8 9 10 11 12 13 14
15 16 17 18 19 20 21	15 16 17 18 19 20 21	15 16 17 18 19 20 21	15 16 17 18 19 20 21	15 16 17 18 19 20 21
22 23 24 25 26 27 28	22 23 24 25 26 27 28	22 23 24 25 26 27 28	22 23 24 25 26 27 28	22 23 24 25 26 27 28
29 30 31	29 30 31	29 30 31	29 30 31	29 30 31
every day	once a week	twice a week	three times a week	once every two weeks

65

How often ...?

1. She eats pizza once a week.

2. three times a week.

3. once every three weeks.

4. two or three times a year.

5. once or twice a month.

6. once every two or three years.

I usually drink dirty water

Horse: How often do you eat out?

Cow: Well, I always eat out in summer.

Horse: What's your favorite restaurant?

Cow: I don't go to restaurants. I eat in a field.

Horse: Uh ... Are you having a nice time?

Cow: Yes, this is great! I'm eating caviar! I usually eat grass for dinner. ... And I'm drinking champagne. I usually drink dirty water.

Pair practice

The students ask and answer questions about eating out (e.g. how often they eat out, what their favorite restaurant is, how often they go to various kinds of restaurants, what they usually eat).

A. Lifestyles

B. How often?

C. Questionnaire (Units 1-15)

15 Consolidation Exercises

1 How often ...?

a. _____

_____

_____

b. _____

_____

_____

c. _____

_____

_____

2 usually / today

a. He usually works in an

office, but today he's

playing golf.

b. _____

_____

_____

_____

c. _____

_____

_____

_____

Questionnaire

How often do you cook?

_____

How often do you speak English?

_____

How often do you go to bed after midnight?

_____

How often do you go to the movies?

_____

How often do you take a vacation?

_____

How often do you eat Chinese food?

_____

Lead-in What's the matter?

Lee: Hi, Marc.
What's the matter?

Marc: I have a headache and
a stomachache.

Lee: Anything else?

Marc: My back hurts.

Lee: Do you smoke?

Marc: Yes, about twenty
cigarettes a day.

Lee: How much do you drink?

Marc: About two bottles of wine
a day.

Lee: Well, you should stop
smoking. And you
shouldn't drink so much.

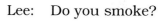

Word building

Manuel has a
headache.

Paula has a
sore throat.

Lee's sister has a
broken leg.

Sachiko's shoulder
hurts.

69

Problems

1

She should
take some medicine.

2

wear glasses.

3

study hard.

4

practice every day.

5

buy a new car.

6

look for a new girlfriend.

Juliet doesn't love me

Dr. Freud:	What's the matter?
Romeo:	Juliet doesn't love me. I think she has a new boyfriend.
Dr. Freud:	How about sending her some flowers?
Romeo:	I send her flowers every day.
Dr. Freud:	How about writing to her?
Romeo:	I write to her three times a day.
Dr. Freud:	How about singing to her?
Romeo:	I sing under her balcony every night.
Dr. Freud:	Who's her new boyfriend?
Romeo:	I'm not sure. I think he's called Casanova.
Dr.Freud:	That's strange. Mrs. Freud has a friend called Casanova, too.

Pair practice

Student A: a psychiatrist   Student B: him/herself or a famous person
Student B has a problem (e.g. doesn't like his/her work, can't sleep, can't stop smoking). Student A gives advice.
Student B should reject Student A's advice in the same way as in the above dialogue.

A. Team advice

B. Good advice?

C. Mime

16 Consolidation Exercises

1 What's the matter?

a. She has _____

_____

_____

b. _____

_____

_____

c. _____

_____

_____

d. _____

_____

_____

2 should / shouldn't

She should/shouldn't _____

_____

_____

_____

_____

_____

3 Dr. Freud

Dr. Freud: What's the matter?

You: _____

_____

Dr. Freud: How about _____

_____?

You: _____

_____

Dr. Freud: How about _____

_____?

You: _____

_____

Questionnaire

How long do you usually sleep?

_____

How long do you usually study/work?

_____

How often do you catch a cold?

_____

How often do you have a headache?

_____

How often do you go to the doctor's?

_____

Lead-in ## I'm flying to Europe next week

Sachiko: David! I have some fantastic news!
I'm flying to Europe next week.

David: That's great!
Where are you going?

Sachiko: On Monday I'm going to London,
and on Thursday I'm going to the
south of France.

David: You're lucky!
I'm working every day next week.

Sachiko: Maybe you can take a vacation next month.

David: I don't think so. I'm teaching
all summer.

Paula: Hi, David!
What are you doing today?

David: Nothing special.

Paula: Lee and I are playing
tennis this afternoon.
Would you like to
come, too?

David: Not really.

Paula: What's the matter?

David: Nothing.

Word building

S M T W T F S	S M T W T F S	S M T W T F S	S M T W T F S	S M T W T F S
1 2 3 4 5 6 7	1 2 3 4 5 6 7	1 2 3 4 5 6 7	1 2 3 4 5 6 7	1 2 3 4 5 6 7
8 9 10 11 12 13 14	8 9 10 11 12 13 14	8 9 10 11 12 13 14	8 9 10 11 12 13 14	8 9 10 11 12 13 14
15 16 17 18 19 20 21	15 16 17 18 19 20 21	15 16 17 18 19 20 21	15 16 17 18 19 20 21	15 16 17 18 19 20 21
22 23 24 25 26 27 28	22 23 24 25 26 27 28	22 23 24 25 26 27 28	22 23 24 25 26 27 28	22 23 24 25 26 27 28
29 30 31	29 30 31	29 30 31	29 30 31	29 30 31
tomorrow	the day after tomorrow	next week	the week after next	three weeks from now

Plans

1

He's playing tennis
on Friday morning.

2

_____
on Friday afternoon.

3

_____
on Friday evening.

4

_____
on Saturday morning.

5

_____
on Saturday afternoon.

6

_____
on Saturday evening.

What are you doing tonight?

Juliet:	Hello.
Romeo:	Hello, Juliet. What are you doing tonight?
Juliet:	I'm going to a concert.
Romeo:	What are you doing tomorrow night?
Juliet:	I'm going to a movie.
Romeo:	What are you doing on Saturday?
Juliet:	I'm going to the beach.
Romeo:	Are you going with Casanova?
Juliet:	Yes, of course.
Romeo:	Oh!
Juliet:	Goodbye!

Pair practice

Students A and B: themselves or famous people.
Student A wants to meet Student B and asks what he/she is doing on the next seven evenings.
Student B doesn't want to meet Student A, and always says he/she is busy, giving a different reason each time.

A. Superstar

B. No pausing

C. Find your partners

Photocopiable

17 Consolidation Exercises

1 What's she doing ...?

... tonight

a. <u>She's going to a</u>
   <u>concert.</u>

... tomorrow morning

b. _____

... tomorrow afternoon

c. _____

... tomorrow night

d. _____

... on Saturday

e. _____

... on Sunday

f. _____

2. Romeo

You: Hello.
Romeo: Hello. What are you doing tonight?
You: _____
          _____

Romeo: What are you doing tomorrow?
You: _____
          _____

Romeo: What are you doing the day after tomorrow?
You: _____
          _____

Romeo: Who are you going with?
You: _____
Romeo: Oh!

Questionnaire

What are you doing tomorrow?

_____

What are you doing the day after tomorrow?

_____

What are you doing next spring?

_____

What are you doing next summer?

_____

What are you doing next fall?

_____

What are you doing next winter?

_____

Lead-in

I'm not going jogging!

Carmen: What do you want to do today?

Manuel: I'd like to go cycling.

Carmen: Cycling! In this weather!
Who do you want to go with?

Manuel: You, of course.

Carmen: Me! You're joking!
I'm not going cycling!
I'm not going jogging!
I'm not going for a walk!
I'm just staying home
in front of the TV!

Carmen: What do you want to do this
evening?

Manuel: I'd like to go out for dinner.

Carmen: Where do you want to go?

Manuel: The restaurant on the top
floor of the Milton Hotel.
It has a beautiful view.

Carmen: And one hamburger's $100!
You're crazy!
Let's just go out for a drink.

Word building

go swimming
(go for a swim)

go cycling
(go for a bike ride)

go for a walk
(take a walk)

go out for a drink
(go drinking)

In Summer

1

She often goes cycling.

2

_____ once or twice a week.

3

_____ never _____

4

_____ three or four times a year.

5

_____ sometimes _____

6

_____ almost every vacation.

Follow-up practice How about going to the U.S.A.?

Travel Agent: How about going to the Riviera?
You can go swimming.
You can go waterskiing.

Columbus: No, I don't want to go to the Riviera.

Travel Agent: How about going to Switzerland?
You can go climbing.
You can go for a picnic in the mountains.

Columbus: No, I don't want to go to Switzerland.

Travel Agent: How about going to the U.S.A.?
You can go surfing.
You can play baseball.
You can visit New York.

Columbus: Uh ... Where is the U.S.A.?

Travel Agent: I don't know.

Columbus: Can I go by ship?

Travel Agent: I think so.

Pair practice

Student A: a travel agent   Student B: him/herself or a famous person
Student A suggests places for Student B to take a vacation, and says what Student B can do in each place.
Student B tries to decide where to go.

78

A. Which country is it?

B. How many questions?

C. World Cup

18 Consolidation Exercises

1 What do they want to do?

a. She wants to go bowling.

b. _____

   _____

c. _____

   _____

2 How often?

How often do you go for a drive?_____

_____

How often do you go jogging?_____

_____

How often do you go fishing?_____

_____

How often do you go for a walk?_____

_____

3 What can we do ...? (go ... -ing / go for ...)

in the mountains: We can go climbing.

   We can go skiing.

at the beach: _____

   _____

in the countryside: _____

   _____

in the city: _____

   _____

4 Columbus

You: May I help you?

Columbus: Yes, I want to take a vacation.

You: How about going to _____?

   You can _____

   You can _____

Columbus: No, I don't want to go to _____

You: How about going to _____?

   You can _____

   You can _____

Columbus: No, I don't want to go to _____

   _____

Questionnaire

What would you like to do tomorrow?

_____

What would you like to do next spring?

_____

What would you like to do next summer?

_____

What would you like to do next fall?

_____

What would you like to do next winter?

_____

Adverbs of manner

good at ◆ bad at

Lead-in ## Marc can swim well

Paula: We're going to the beach this week-end. Would you like to come, too?

David: Are Sachiko and Marc going?

Paula: Yes, of course. Why?

David: I bet Marc can swim well, can dive well ... and I bet he can surf well, too!

Paula: It doesn't matter.

David: Yes, it does. I can't swim very well, I can't dive, and I surf very badly.

Paula: David! Do you like Sachiko?

David: Who? Me?

Sachiko: Are you good at putting up tents?

David: Well, I go camping a lot.

Sachiko: So, please come with us!

David: I'm sorry Sachiko.
I don't like the beach very much.
And I'm very bad at swimming.

Sachiko: Don't worry.
We can go for a long walk together.

David: A long walk? ... Well ... uh ... Yes ...
I'm pretty good at putting up tents.
And I'm a great cook!

Word building

Carmen's good at singing.

Manuel's bad at singing.

Paula knows a lot about cars.

Marc doesn't know anything about cars.

Adverbs

1

She's running very fast (quickly).

2

_____ slowly.

3

_____ quietly.

4

_____ snoring _____ loudly.

5

_____ carelessly.

6

_____ carefully.

Jump!

Pirates:	Jump!
Man:	Uh ... I can paint the ship. I can paint beautifully! How about a purple mast?
Pirates:	Jump!
Man:	... I can run fast.
Pirates:	On a ship? Jump!
Man:	... I can sing.
Captain:	Can you sing "I Am Sailing"?
Man:	Oh yes! I can sing it really softly and romantically ... "I am sailing, I am sailing ..."
Captain:	That's terrible! Don't sing so loudly!
Man:	"... Home again, across the sea."
Captain:	Stop! Stop! OK. Don't jump!
Shark:	I'm not hungry anyway.

Pair practice

Student A: the pirate captain saying "Jump" or "OK. Don't Jump" to Student B.
Student B: him/herself or a famous person on the plank of the pirate ship. He/she has to give a good reason for not having to jump, using the pattern "I can + adverb of manner".

A. Guess who

B. Leaving the room

C. Mime

19 Consolidation Exercises

1 well / badly

How well can you speak English?

Very well. _____

How well can you cook?

_____

How well can you sing?

_____

How well can you use a word processor?

_____

2 What are they doing?

a. *He's playing baseball badly.* _____

b. _____

c. _____

d. _____

e. _____

f. _____

3 Jump!

Pirates: Jump!

You: *I can run fast.* _____

Pirates: Jump!

You: _____

Pirates: Jump!

You: _____

Pirates: Jump!

You: _____

Pirates: Jump!

You: _____

Pirates: OK. Don't jump.

You: Thank you.

Questionnaire

What do you do well?

_____

What do you do badly?

_____

What do you do slowly?

_____

What do you do quickly?

_____

What do you do quietly?

_____

What do you do loudly?

_____

What do you do carefully?

_____

What do you do carelessly?

_____

All · most · some · none

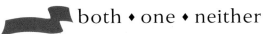

both · one · neither

Lead-in ## Are any of you thirsty?

David and his class are camping on the beach. All of them are having a good time. Some of them are swimming, and some of them are lying on the beach.

Sachiko:	Are any of you thirsty?
Marc:	Yes, I'd like a cool drink.
Sachiko:	Me too. There's a store over there. Could you get me some orange juice?
Paula:	And could you get me an ice cream?
Manuel:	And could you get me a beer?
Marc:	Do any of you want to come, too?
All:	No, thank you!

Sachiko:	I'm hungry! Let's make a fire and cook lunch.
Marc:	We can go to a restaurant.
Sachiko:	There aren't any restaurants near here.
Manuel:	We can eat later. Some of us want to swim. And none of us want to cook.
Paula:	Most of us are very hungry!
Manuel:	Oh all right. Let's make a fire.

Word building

Paula's hungry.

David's sad.

Carmen's tired.

Sachiko's angry.

all / most / some

1

All of them are vampires.

2

_____ vampires.

3

_____ vampires.

4

_____ vampires.

5

Both _____ vampires.

6

Neither _____ vampires.

Where's Scarface?

Policeman: OK Luigi. Both of us are very busy, and we don't have time to play games.
Where's Scarface?

Luigi: _Non parlo inglese._

Policeman: Listen, Luigi!
Neither of us are stupid. I know you can speak English.

Luigi: _Non capisco!_

Policeman: This is taking a long time!
I'm hungry ... This hot dog looks good.

Luigi: _Fami mangiare!_

Policeman: Well, only one of us can eat it.
Look! There's a note on it.
It says "With love from Scarface".
That's very kind of him!

BANG!

Luigi: _Mama mia!_ Not again!

Policeman: So you **can** speak English!

Pair practice

Students A and B: themselves or famous people
The students decide who they are, and then try to make sentences about themselves using the patterns
"Both of us ...", "Neither of us ...", and "One of us ...".

A. Sentences

B. Pairs

C. Dominoes

20 Consolidation Exercises

1 both / one / neither

a. <u>Both of them have four legs.</u>

b. _____

c. _____

d. _____

e. _____

f. _____

2 Your class / Your family

My class		My family	
All of us _____		All of us _____	
Most _____		Most _____	
Some _____		Some _____	
One _____		One _____	
None _____		None _____	

Questionnaire

What do you think all of your class would like to do next Sunday?

_____

_____

What do you think most of your class would like to do next Sunday?

_____

_____

What do you think all of your class would like to do next summer?

_____

_____

What do you think most of your class would like to do next summer?

_____

_____

Lead-in ## First, we make the fire

Sachiko: Right! It's time to cook lunch.

Marc: Uh ... What do we do?

David: It's easy.
First, we make the fire.
Then, we boil some water.
Then, we put the curry bags in the water.

Sachiko: How about the rice?

David: We boil that, too.

Sachiko: OK! Let's get going!

Marc: Uh ... How do we make the fire?

David: It isn't difficult.
First, we dig a hole.
Then, we put some rocks around the hole.

Sachiko: What do we do after that?

David: We put some paper in the hole.
Then, we put some wood on the paper.
Then, we light the fire.

Word building

boil

fry

barbecue

bake

How to get to sleep

First, get into bed.

First, start the engine

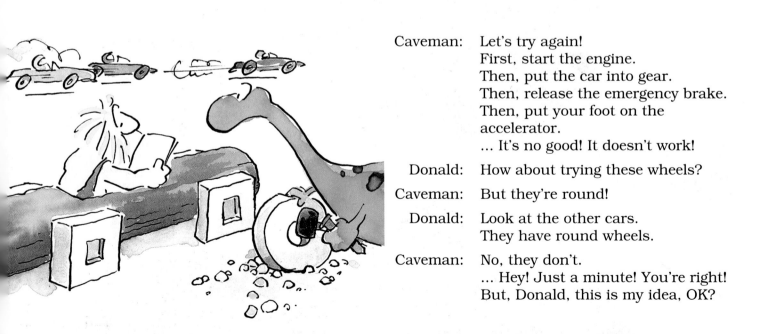

Caveman: Let's try again!
First, start the engine.
Then, put the car into gear.
Then, release the emergency brake.
Then, put your foot on the accelerator.
... It's no good! It doesn't work!

Donald: How about trying these wheels?

Caveman: But they're round!

Donald: Look at the other cars.
They have round wheels.

Caveman: No, they don't.
... Hey! Just a minute! You're right!
But, Donald, this is my idea, OK?

Pair practice

Student A explains how to make or do something (e.g. cook something, draw a picture, find a job, make something out of paper, wash your hair). Student B offers suggestions.

Communication Activities 21

A. Routines

B. Miming sequences

C. How do you ...?

21 Consolidation Exercises

1 How to make a telephone call

a. First, pick up the telephone receiver.

b. _____

c. _____

2 How to use a dryer

  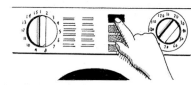

a. _____

b. _____

c. _____

3 How to mail a letter

  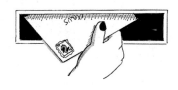

Santa Claus

a. _____

b. _____

c. _____

4 How to cook ...

How to cook

_____

_____

_____

_____

_____

_____

_____

_____

_____

Questionnaire

What do you usually do in the morning?

First, I _____

_____

_____

What do you usually do in the afternoon?

_____

_____

_____

What do you usually do in the evening?

_____

_____

_____

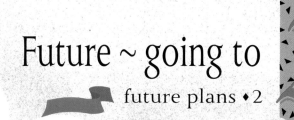

Future ~ going to

future plans ♦ 2

Lead-in What are they going to do in August?

Kim's going to fly to Egypt. He's going to visit the Pyramids and sail down The Nile. He's going to stay there for six days.

Manuel and Carmen are going to go to Canada for ten days. They're going to go cycling in the Rockies. They're going to cycle thirty kilometers a day.

Michelle isn't going to take a vacation. She's going to take an important exam in September, so she's going to study hard every day.

Word building After ... going to ...

graduate from college

save money

get married

93

Plans

1

He's going to watch a video tonight.

2

_____
tomorrow morning.

3

_____
three days from now.

4

_____
after they get married.

5

_____
after she graduates.

6

_____
after he goes back to France.

Dinosaur steak

Caveman: What are you going to do after you leave the hospital?

Reporter: I'm going to go shopping.

Caveman: What are you going to buy?

Reporter: I'm going to buy a gun.

Caveman: What are you going to do after that?

Reporter: I'm going to eat a big dinner.

Caveman: What are you going to eat?

Reporter: Dinosaur steak!

Pair practice

Student A: him/herself   Student B: him/herself or a famous person
Student A asks Student B a "going to" question (e.g. "What are you going to do on Sunday?").
Student B either gives true answers, or plays the role of a famous person. Student A asks follow-up "going to" questions.

A. Consequences

B. Crystal ball

C. Palmistry

22 Consolidation Exercises

1 What's she going to do next week?

a. On Sunday

b. Monday

c. Tuesday

d. Wednesday

e. Thursday

f. Friday

g. Saturday

2 Your family and friends

Me			
going to			

Questionnaire

What are you going to do tomorrow?

What are you going to do next year?

What are you going to do the day after tomorrow?

What are you going to do after you save some money?

What are you going to do next week?

What are you doing to do after you graduate from school/retire from your job?

Lead-in

I have to go to the doctor's

Manuel: We're only going away for ten days!

Carmen: I know! But, we have to take some clothes.

Manuel: Yes, but we don't have to take any books!

Carmen: I like reading on vacation.

Manuel: We're going cycling.
Books are very heavy!

Carmen: Oh, all right.

Manuel: Help! Look at the time!

Carmen: What's the matter?

Manuel: I have to get some Canadian dollars.

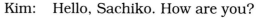

Kim: Hello, Sachiko. How are you?

Sachiko: Very busy! I'm leaving for Europe
tomorrow morning.
And I have to go to the doctor's,
I have to go to the beauty salon,
I have to go shopping ...

Kim: What do you have to buy?

Sachiko: I have to buy a camera, some
new shoes, a swimsuit ...

Kim: But you have a nice swimsuit.

Sachiko: It isn't nice! It's old!

Word building

dollars
cents

pounds
pence

marks
pfennigs

have to

1

2

3

He has to get up in the
middle of the night.

_____

_____

4

5

6

_____

_____

_____

_____

_____

_____

I have to work at night

Mrs. Dracula: I'm tired! I have to get up at six
o'clock every day.
I have to cook.
I have to wash the dishes.
I have to clean the house.
You never help me!

Dracula: I have to work, dear.

Mrs. Dracula: Work! You don't work!
You stay in bed all day!
And you stay out all night!
You always come home at six
o'clock in the morning.

Dracula: I have to work at night, dear.

Mrs. Dracula: Huh!

Pair practice

The students tell each other about the things they have to do every day.

A. Newspaper reporters

B. What's my job?

C. Grand Prix

23 Consolidation Exercises

1 Yes, I do. / No, I don't.

Do you have to study/work hard?

_____

Do you usually have to get up before seven o'clock?

_____

Do you usually have to cook dinner?

_____

Do you usually have to wash the dishes?

_____

2 In the office

a. She has to answer the telephone.

b. _____
   _____

c. _____
   _____

d. _____
   financial reports.

3 What do they have to do?

policemen and policewomen
They have to wear uniforms.

English teachers
_____

taxi drivers
_____

pilots
_____

marathon runners
_____

office workers
_____

Questionnaire

What do you have to do?

1. _____
   _____

2. _____
   _____

3. _____
   _____

4. _____
   _____

What don't you have to do?

1. _____
   _____

2. _____
   _____

3. _____
   _____

4. _____
   _____

Lead-in ## She has dark hair

Manuel: Excuse me.
I'm looking for my wife.

Pilot: What does she look like?

Manuel: She has dark hair and brown eyes, and she's quite tall. She's wearing a white T-shirt and a yellow skirt.

Pilot: Is that her over there?

Manuel: Yes, it is.
Thank you very much.

Marc: Hello, Carmen.
Have a good time in Canada.

Carmen: Hi, Marc!
What are you doing here?

Marc: I'm saying goodbye to Sachiko.

Carmen: Oh yes, your girlfriend.
I don't know her very well.
What's she like?

Marc: She's quite nice,
but she's bad-tempered.
And she's not really my girlfriend.

Sachiko: Marc!

Marc: Oh! Hi, Sachiko.

Word building

Manuel
has a beard.

Marc
has a mustache.

Michelle's
wearing glasses.

Carmen's
wearing earrings.

What does he/she look like? ◆ What's he/she like?

1

She has black hair
and I think she's

_____

2

_____
_____
_____

3

_____
_____
_____

4

_____
_____
_____

5

_____
_____
_____

6

_____
_____
_____

bad-tempered   active   selfish   serious   shy   cool   kind   honest   friendly

Mr. Universe

Announcer: Ladies and gentlemen.
Welcome to the Mr. Universe
contest!

The first contestant is Hic from
Pluto. Hic has a beautiful long
neck, fantastic blue hair, and a
lovely tail. Thank you Hic.

The second contestant is Atchoo
from Planet A-A-Atchoo.
Wow! Look at his shirt!
It's from Earth!
And it only has two sleeves!
I think it's going to be the new
fashion!

Pair practice

The students talk about what they and the other students in the class look like and what they are wearing. If
appropriate, they can imagine they are taking part in a fashion contest.

A. Pictures of people

B. Criminals

C. The Zodiac

24 Consolidation Exercises

1 What do they look like?

a. _____
_____

b. _____

c. _____

2 Your family and friends

```
_____



She has _____


_____


I think she's _____


_____
```

```
_____



_____


_____


_____


_____
```

```
_____



_____


_____


_____


_____
```

3 Animals

What do giraffes look like?

_____

_____

What do pandas look like?

_____

_____

What do tigers look like?

_____

_____

What do zebras look like?

_____

Questionnaire

What does your favorite singer look like?

_____

_____

What does your favorite sportsman/woman look like?

_____

_____

What's your English teacher like?

_____

_____

What's the President/Prime Minister of your country like?

_____

_____

Lead-in

What's London like?

Paula: Hello.

Sachiko: Paula? Is that you?

Paula: Yes. How are you Sachiko?

Sachiko: Tired!

Paula: What's London like?

Sachiko: It's great! There are a lot of parks. And the stores are fantastic!

Paula: Are you having a good time?

Sachiko: Well, I'm working most of the time. But, I'm going to a concert tomorrow night.

Paula: What's the weather like?

Sachiko: Terrible! It's raining all the time.

Paula: It's beautiful here. It's sunny and hot every day.

Sachiko: Thanks a lot!

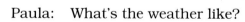

Word building

It's cloudy.

It's windy.

It's freezing.

It's humid.

Around the world

New York

Sahara

What's New York like?
It's very big and there are
a lot of tall buildings.

_____?
_____

Amazon

Himalayas

_____?
_____
_____

_____?
_____
_____

You should stay in Siberia

Donald: What's the weather like in Siberia?

Mammoth: It's freezing!
It snows all the time and there's a
lot of ice. It's usually warm in June!
I want to take a vacation!
What's the weather like in Mexico
in July?

Donald: It's usually very nice. We can
usually lie on the beach or go
swimming in the sea.
But, this year I think it's going to
be very, very hot!
You should stay in Siberia.

Pair practice

Student B says one or two places he/she knows. Student A asks Student B "What's the weather like in (place) in (month)?" Student B answers and says something about the place at that time of year (e.g. "We can usually …").

A. Where am I?

B. A place you know well

C. World strategy game

25 Consolidation Exercises

1 What's ... like?

2 What's the weather like?

What's the weather like in California in summer?

I think _____

What's the weather like in Siberia in winter?

_____

What's the weather like in Japan in summer?

_____

What's the weather like at the North Pole in winter?

_____

3 He/She should ...

Questionnaire

Where do you live?

_____

What's it like?

_____

What's the weather like in spring?

_____

What's the weather like in summer?

_____

What's the weather like in fall?

_____

What's the weather like in winter?

_____

What country would you like to visit?

_____

Why?

_____

Lead-in ## I'm in better shape than you

Manuel: Come on, Carmen!
We can't stop every ten minutes!

Carmen: Well, don't go so fast!
You're bigger than me!
You're stronger than me!
And your bike's much better
than mine!

Manuel: You're out of shape.
You should do more exercise.

Carmen: I'm in better shape than you!
You never do any exercise.

Manuel: Yes, but you're tired, not me.
You're out of shape and you're
putting on weight!

Carmen: Manuel!
You're much fatter than me!
I'm going home!!

Word building

Michelle's
in good shape.

David's
out of shape.

Marc's
putting on weight.

Paula's
losing weight.

taller than

1

2

3

He's taller than her.   _____ him.   _____

4

5

6

_____   _____   _____

happier   thinner   ~~taller~~   stronger   younger   lazier

Follow-up practice   # Is he better looking than me?

Juliet:	Hello.
Romeo:	Hello. This is Romeo again. What are you doing today?
Juliet:	I'm going to the beach with Casanova.
Romeo:	... Is Casanova good looking?
Juliet:	Yes, he's very good looking.
Romeo:	Is he better looking than me?
Juliet:	Oh, yes! He's much better looking than you.
Romeo:	Is he taller than me?
Juliet:	No, he isn't.
Romeo:	Is he richer than me?
Juliet:	Romeo! Casanova's my new dog! Goodbye!

Pair practice

Student A thinks of a person who Student B knows and says if it's a "he"or a "she". Student B tries to find out who the person is, using questions which include a comparison. If an answer is "yes", Student B can guess who the person is. The students take turns and the one with the least guesses wins.

A. Put them in order

B. Sevens

C. Twenty questions

26 Consolidation Exercises

1 Which is ... -er?

a. <u>The businessman is taller than</u>
   <u>the cook.</u>

b. <u>The car</u>

c. <u>The student</u>

d. <u>The fish</u>

e. <u>The robber</u>

f. <u>The elephant</u>

2 Quiz

a. **Which is longer, the Nile or the Mississippi?**
<u>   is longer than</u>

b. **Which is larger, Sydney or Paris?**

c. **Which is higher, Mont Blanc or Mount Fuji?**

d. **Which is older, the Golden Gate Bridge in San Francisco or the Statue of Liberty in New York?**

Questionnaire

Who is taller than you?

<u>   is taller than me.</u>

Who is shorter than you?

Who is stronger than you?

Who is lazier than you?

Who is happier than you?

Who can run faster than you?

Who is in better shape than you?

Who has longer hair than you?

Lead-in I like Nice better than London

Dear David,

I'm in Nice in the south of France. I'm lying on the beach. The sea is beautiful and the weather is great! I like Nice better than London — I don't have to carry an umbrella every day!

London is bigger and more exciting than Nice. There are more stores, more concert halls, and more theaters. But, Nice is cleaner than London, and the weather is much better!

I'm looking forward to seeing you soon.

With love from,

Sachiko

Word building

Sincerely,

Kim Jin Woo

Kim Jin Woo
Sales Manager

Yours,

Paula

Best Wishes

David

with love

Michelle

more ... than

1

Chinese is more difficult
than English.

2

Tigers _____

3

The car _____

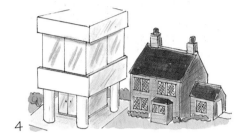

4

The house on the left _____
_____

5

Cities _____
_____

6

Gorillas _____
_____

polluted   expensive   difficult   dangerous   intelligent   modern

Follow-up practice It's more fun than lying in a bath all day

Reporter: Well, Julius.
Which do you like better, New York
or Rome?

Julius: Oh, New York! Rome is much
more polluted than New York.

Reporter: More polluted! But, in New York
there are so many cars and trucks!
In Rome you only have horses.

Julius: Yes, I know. So the streets are very
dirty! And we can't walk around in
sandals.

Reporter: I see. That's very interesting.

Julius: And New York is more exciting!

Reporter: Really?

Julius: Oh yes! Watching the New York
Yankees is much more fun than
lying in a bath all day.

Pair practice

Student A: a reporter   Student B: him/herself or a famous person
Student A asks Student B which of two places he/she likes better, and encourages him/her to give reasons.

Communication Activities 27

A. Boasting

B. What is it?

C. Comparing countries

27 Consolidation Exercises

1 Which do you like better?

Which do you like better, jazz or classical music?

_____

_____

Which do you like better, the beach or the park?

_____

_____

2 Which is more ...?

a. _She is more popular_
   than him.

b. _____
   expensive _____

c. _____
   intelligent _____

3 Which do you think ...?

Which do you think is more difficult, Chinese or English?

I think Chinese is more difficult than English.

_____

Which do you think are more dangerous, alligators or lions?

_____

_____

Which do you think are more exciting, discos or rock concerts?

_____

_____

Which do you think is more interesting, watching movies or reading?

_____

_____

4 A postcard

Questionnaire

Who is more bad-tempered than you?

_____

Who is more selfish than you?

_____

Who is busier than you?

_____

Who speaks English better than you?

_____

Lead-in ## When did Cleopatra live?

Kim: When did Cleopatra live?

Guide: She lived about 2,000 years ago.

Kim: Why is she so famous?

Guide: Well, she was very beautiful, and two famous Romans loved her – Julius Caesar and Mark Anthony.

Kim: Did she marry one of them?

Guide: No, she didn't.
She married her brother.

Kim: Her brother!

Guide: Yes, but she went to Rome with Julius Caesar.

Kim: Did she come back to Egypt?

Guide: Yes, and Mark Anthony came here, too. But, Rome attacked Egypt, and Mark Anthony killed himself. So Cleopatra killed herself, too.

Word building

S M T W T F S	S M T W T F S	S M T W T F S	S M T W T F S	S M T W T F S
1 2 3 4 5 6 7	1 2 3 4 5 6 7	1 2 3 4 5 6 7	①②③④⑤⑥⑦	1 2 3 ④ 5 6 7
8 9⑩11 12 13 14	8 ⑨10 11 12 13 14	⑧ 9 10 11 12 13 14	8 9 10 11 12 13 14	8 9 10 11 12 13 14
15 16 17 18 19 20 21	15 16 17 18 19 20 21	15 16 17 18 19 20 21	15 16 17 18 19 20 21	15 16 17 18 19 20 21
22 23 24 25 26 27 28	22 23 24 25 26 27 28	22 23 24 25 26 27 28	22 23 24 25 26 27 28	22 23 24 25 26 27 28
29 30 31	29 30 31	29 30 31	29 30 31	29 30 31
yesterday	the day before yesterday	three days ago	last week	two weeks ago

Last year

1

He smoked 30 cigarettes a day.

2

_____ seven hours a day.

3

_____ work or study.

4

_____ every night.

5

And _____ do any exercise.

6

But, this year he wants to win an Olympic medal.

I came to Earth in a UFO

Dr. Freud:	Where were you born?
Atchoo:	On Planet A-A-Atchoo.
Dr. Freud:	What schools did you go to?
Atchoo:	I went to Choo City Junior and Senior High Schools.
Dr. Freud:	What subjects did you like at school?
Atchoo:	Earth history and time travel.
Dr. Freud:	What did you do after leaving school?
Atchoo:	I came to Earth in a UFO.
Dr.Freud:	And what are your ambitions?
Atchoo:	I want to marry a girl with two heads and five arms, and I want to travel around the universe with her.
Dr. Freud:	So what's the matter?
Atchoo:	I get travel sick.

Pair practice

Student A: a psychiatrist   Student B: him/herself, alien, or a famous person
Student A asks the same questions as in the dialogue, and other similar questions he/she knows or can guess
how to say. Student B either gives true answers, or plays the role of an alien or a famous person.

A. Photographs and pictures

B. Who was I?

C. Last sentence

28 Consolidation Exercises

1 What did they do last Sunday?

a. He played tennis.
_____

b. _____

c. _____

d. _____
_____

e. _____

f. _____

2 Quiz

a. Who was the first President of the U.S.A.?
George Washington
_____

b. Who had a hit record called *"Hey Jude"*?
_____

c. Who sailed to the New World in 1492?
_____

d. Who was the first man on the moon?
_____

e. Who painted the Mona Lisa?
_____

f. Who did Romeo love?
_____

3 A famous person

_____
_____
_____
_____
_____
_____
_____
_____
_____
_____
_____

Questionnaire

Where were you born?
_____

What schools did/do you go to?
_____

What did you/are you going to do after finishing school?
_____

What are your ambitions?
_____
_____

Past simple ·2·

vacations

29

Lead-in   Sachiko had a great time in Europe

Sachiko had a great time in Europe. She visited London and Nice. She stayed in London for three days and then she went to Nice for four days.

In London, she visited Westminster Abbey, the Tower of London and the British Museum, and she took a lot of photographs. She went shopping on Oxford Street and Regent Street, and she bought a lot of clothes. She also went to a very exciting rock concert at Wembley Stadium.

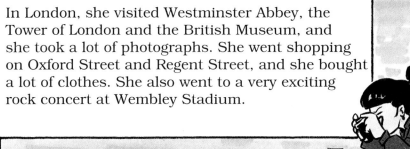

In Nice, she lay on the beach and got very brown. She went waterskiing and windsurfing, and she went for a long walk. She met some French college students on the beach, and they went to a disco together. She ate a lot of delicious food and she drank a lot of French wine.

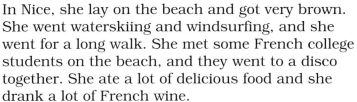

Word building   Last Saturday night

Carmen met some new friends.

Manuel wrote a letter.

Lee bought a ring for Paula.

David taught English.

121

Last night

1 He left Egypt.

2 __ some interesting people.

3 __ a big bowl of spaghetti.

4 _____ very well.

5 __ a letter to her parents.

6 _____ a lot of tequila.

What was the U.S.A. like?

Travel Agent:	What was the U.S.A. like?
Columbus:	Fantastic!
Travel Agent:	How long were you there?
Columbus:	About two weeks.
Travel Agent:	What was the weather like?
Columbus:	Great! It was sunny all the time.
Travel Agent:	What did you do?
Columbus:	I hunted buffalo. I looked for gold. And I visited the White House.
Travel Agent:	Where would you like to go next year?
Columbus:	I want to sail around the world.
Travel Agent:	Around the world! You can't! The world is flat.
Columbus:	No, it isn't! It's round!
Travel Agent:	Oh, well. You should talk to Mr. Magellan. He's planning a round-the-world cruise, too.

Pair practice

Student A: a travel agent   Student B: him/herself or a famous person
Student B has just returned from a holiday (real or imagined). Student A asks the questions in the dialogue and other similar questions he/she knows or can guess how to say.

A. Where was my vacation?

B. Chain story

C. Picture story

29 Consolidation Exercises

1 What did they do on vacation?

a. <u>He took some</u>
   <u>photographs.</u>

b. _____
   _____

c. _____
   _____

d. _____
   _____

e. _____
   _____

f. _____
   _____

2 What did your family and friends do last Sunday?

a. <u>I think my sister stayed home.</u> _____

b. _____
   _____

c. _____
   _____

d. _____
   _____

3 Last week

go	<u>I went to a concert.</u> _____
buy	_____
make	_____
meet	_____
write	_____
see	_____
take	_____

Questionnaire

Where did you go last year?

_____

What was it like?

_____

How long were you there?

_____

What was the weather like?

_____

What did you eat?

_____

What did you drink?

_____

What did you buy?

_____

Who did you meet?

_____

Had to · wanted · could

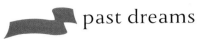 past dreams

Lead-in ## I had to smile all the time

Paula: Did you have a nice flight?

Sachiko: No, it was terrible.
I had to work so hard!

Paula: What did you have to do?

Sachiko: I had to take care of the passengers.
I had to walk up and down the plane.
I had to smile all the time ...

Paula: Could you sleep?

Sachiko: No. I wanted to sleep, but I couldn't.

Paula: Could you sit down?

Sachiko: Yes, but only for ten minutes.
I was so busy!

David: Sachiko! Welcome back!

Sachiko: David! I bought a souvenir for you.
Here you are.

David: Wow! An England soccer uniform!
Thanks, Sachiko!

Marc: How about me?

Sachiko: Oh, Marc! I'm sorry!
I wanted to buy you a jacket,
but I completely forgot.
Maybe Carmen bought you one.

Word building ## Ten years ago

Carmen wanted to be
a politician.

David wanted to be
a soccer player.

Sachiko wanted to be
an actress.

Marc wanted to be
a bank manager.

Yesterday ...

1

He had to clean his apartment.

2

_____his clothes.

3

_____his clothes.

4

_____dinner.

5

_____by himself.

6

_____the dishes.

I wanted to be an English teacher

Reporter: Why did you become a pirate?

Captain: That's a difficult question. At school, I wanted to be an English teacher.

Reporter: An English teacher!

Captain: Yes, but just after high school I came to the Caribbean on vacation. It was a fantastic vacation! I could go swimming, I could go surfing ... and I didn't have to study.

Reporter: But, why did you become a pirate?

Captain: I got married, so I had to get a steady job. It's a little dangerous, but the pay's good.

Pair practice

Student A: a reporter   Student B: him/herself or a famous person
Student A asks questions about Student B's life (e.g. "What high school did you go to?"), and then asks reasons why Student B did certain things in his/her life (e.g. "Why did you go to ... high school?").

A. Name a time

B. True / False

C. Questionnaire (Units 1-30)

30 Consolidation Exercises

1 Yes, I did. / No, I didn't.

Did you have to work/study hard yesterday?

_____

_____

Did you want to stay out later last night?

_____

_____

Did you have to cook dinner last night?

_____

_____

Did you want to take a longer vacation last year?

_____

_____

2 Then and now

10 years ago

a. _She had to get up_
   at seven o'clock.

b. _____

c. _____

Yesterday

d. _____

e. _____

f. _____

Questionnaire

Ten years ago:

What did you have to do?

_____

What didn't you have to do?

_____

What could you do?

_____

What couldn't you do?

_____

What did you want to become?

_____

What didn't you want to become?

_____

Yesterday:

What did you have to do?

_____

What didn't you have to do?

_____

What did you want to do?

_____

What didn't you want to do?

_____

Grammar and Usage

The students work through these exercises and build their own grammar and usage reference.

1	Nationalities	**8**	Present continuous	**15**	All ...
2	Yes/No questions	**9**	Present simple	**16**	Future (-ing • going to)
3	Prepositions	**10**	Transportation	**17**	After ...
4	Numbers	**11**	Adverbs of frequency	**18**	like
5	Countable • uncountable	**12**	Contrasting the present tenses	**19**	Comparatives
6	Possessive pronouns	**13**	You should • How about?	**20**	Past simple
7	Music • Sports	**14**	Adverbs of manner		

1 Nationalities

a. David's from the U.S.A.   _He's American._   b. Sachiko's from Japan.   _She's Japanese._

c. Kim's from Korea.   _____   d. Lee's from China.   _____

e. Carmen's from Mexico.   _____   f. Paula's from Brazil.   _____

g. Michelle's from Switzerland.   _____   h. Marc's from France.   _____

Answers: c. He's Korean.   d. He's Chinese.   e. She's Mexican.   f. She's Brazilian.   g. She's Swiss.   h. He's French.

2 Yes/No questions

a. Is Michelle from Switzerland?   _Yes, she is._   b. Is Carmen Spanish?   _No, she isn't._

c. Are you wearing a skirt?   _____   d. Are you watching TV?   _____

e. Do you like your job/school?   _____   f. Is there a gym near your house? _____

g. Does your boss have long hair?   _____   h. Are there any cats in your room? _____

3 Prepositions

I live in _____

I live next to _____

I live near _____

I live across from _____

4 Numbers

1	_one_	1st	_first_	6	_____	6th	_____
2	_____	2nd	_____	7	_____	7th	_____
3	_____	3rd	_____	8	_____	8th	_____
4	_____	4th	_____	9	_____	9th	_____
5	_____	5th	_____	10	_____	10th	_____

Answers: 1 - one, first   2 - two, second   3 - three, third   4 - four, fourth   5 - five, fifth   6 - six, sixth   7 - seven, seventh   8 - eight, eighth   9 - nine, ninth   10 - ten, tenth

129

Grammar and Usage

5 Countable • uncountable

A. (some • any • a • an)

a. <u>There's some</u> _____ milk.
b. <u>There aren't any</u> _____ eggs.
c. _____ champagne.
d. _____ orange.
e. _____ bread.
f. _____ bananas.
g. _____ pineapples.
h. _____ vase.
i. _____ yogurt.
j. _____ flowers.
k. _____ melon.
l. _____ spoons.

Answers: c. There's some champagne. d. There's an orange. e. There isn't any bread. f. There are some bananas. g. There aren't any pineapples. h. There's a vase. i. There isn't any yogurt. j. There are some flowers. k. There's a melon. l. There aren't any spoons.

B. (quantities of uncountable nouns)

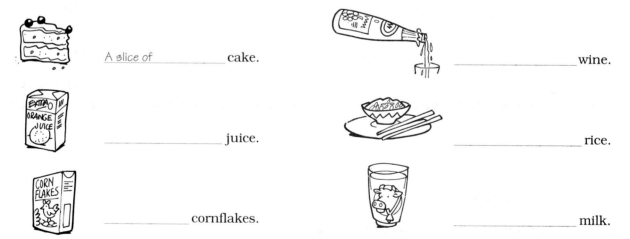

<u>A slice of</u> _____ cake.

_____ wine.

_____ juice.

_____ rice.

_____ cornflakes.

_____ milk.

Answers: A bottle of wine. A carton of juice. A bowl of rice. A box of cornflakes. A glass of milk.

6 Possessive pronoun

a. These are my socks. <u>These are mine.</u>
b. Those are her earrings. _____
c. Those are your gloves. _____
d. These are our pajamas. _____
e. Those are his jeans. _____
f. Those are their shoes. _____

Answers: b. Those are hers. c. Those are yours. d. These are ours. e. Those are his. f. Those are theirs.

7 Music • Sports

a. Manuel __can play the__ piano. b. David _____ soccer. c. Sachiko _____ tennis.

d. Paula _____ paint. e. Carmen _____ sail. f. Marc _____ guitar.

Answers: b. can play c. can play d. can e. can f. can play the

8 Present continuous

go	_going_	study	_____	run	_____	come	_____
play	_____	think	_____	sit	_____	make	_____
eat	_____	listen	_____	get	_____	give	_____
read	_____	watch	_____	put	_____	have	_____

Answers: study-studying, run-running, come-coming, play-playing, sit-sitting, think-thinking, make-making, eat-eating, listen-listening, get-getting, give-giving, read-reading, watch-watching, put-putting, have-having

9 Present simple

A.

like	_likes_	have	_____	make	_____	teach	_____
go	_____	watch	_____	love	_____	write	_____
want	_____	eat	_____	study	_____	put	_____

Answers: like-likes, have-has, make-makes, teach-teaches, go-goes, watch-watches, love-loves, write-writes, want-wants, eat-eats, study-studies, put-puts

B. (general statements)

a. He's a policeman.   He wears a uniform.

b. She's a doctor.   She works in a hospital.

c. He's an artist.   _____

d. She's a student.   _____

e. She's a secretary.   _____

f. He's a businessman.   _____

g. He's a baseball player.   _____

h. She's a pilot.   _____

Grammar and Usage

10 Transportation

a.

She   **drives**   to work.

She goes to work by car.

b.

_____ rides _____

_____

c.

_____ takes _____

_____

d.

_____ walks _____

_____

Answers: b. He rides a bicycle to work./He goes to work by bicycle.   c. He takes a train to work./He goes to work by train.
d. She walks to work./She goes to work on foot.

11 Adverbs of frequency

I	always	_____ go bowling _____	_____ on Sunday evening. _____
I	usually		
I	often		
I	sometimes		
I	never		

I	_____	every day.
I	_____	once or twice a week.
I	_____	once every two weeks.

12 Contrasting the present tenses

a.

She usually drinks
orange juice, *but tonight*
she's drinking vodka.

b.

hard, _____
_____
_____

c.

on Monday morning,_____
_____
_____

d.

home,_____
_____
_____ a good time.

Answers: b. He usually works hard, but today he's lying on the beach.   **c.** He usually works on Monday morning, but today he's sleeping.   **d.** She usually stays home, but today she's having a good time.

13 You should ◆ How about

> I'm very tired.

You: You should _____
_____
You: How about _____?
_____

> I don't like my job.

You: You should _____
_____
You: How about _____?
_____

> My English is terrible.

You: You should _____
_____
You: How about _____?
_____

> I don't have any money.

You: You should _____
_____
You: How about _____?
_____

Grammar and Usage

14 Adverbs of manner

slow	_slowly_	beautiful	_____	bad	_____
quiet	_____	hard	_____	careful	_____
good	_____	loud	_____	fast	_____
romantic	_____	careless	_____	terrible	_____

15 All ...

a.

All of them are _____ bananas.

b.

_____ bananas.

c.

_____ bananas.

d.

_____ bananas.

e.

_____ bananas.

f.

_____ bananas.

g.

_____ a banana.

16 Future (-ing • going to)

a. *Tomorrow morning*

    (-ing)   I'm playing tennis tomorrow
                morning.

  (going to) I'm going to play tennis tomorrow
                morning.

b. *Next week*

    (-ing)

  (going to)

c. *The day after tomorrow*

    (-ing)

  (going to)

d. *Next month*

    (-ing)

  (going to)

17 After ...

a. she / married / big house (going to)

After she gets married, she's going to live in a big house.

b. he / graduates / college / teacher (going to)

c. she finishes her exams / Hawaii (going to *or* -ing)

Answers: b. After he graduates from college, he's going to be a teacher.
c. After she finishes her exams, she's going to Hawaii (she's going to go to Hawaii).

18 like

a. What sport do you like?

b. What sport does your teacher/boss like?

c. What are you like?

d. What's your teacher/boss like?

e. What do you look like?

f. What does your teacher/boss look like?

Grammar and Usage

19 Comparatives

A. (-er)

+ er		+ r	
cheap	cheaper	close	closer
clean	cleaner	large	
cold	colder	nice	
fast	faster	safe	
hard		**gg/tt/nn + er**	
high		big	bigger
kind		fat	
long		hot	
loud		thin	
low		**ẏ + ier**	
new		angry	angrier
old		busy	
quiet		dirty	
rich		easy	
short		happy	
slow		hungry	
small		lazy	
strong		noisy	
tall		shy	
weak		thirsty	
young			

B. (more ...)

beautiful	more beautiful	famous	
boring		intelligent	
dangerous		interesting	
delicious		modern	
difficult		polluted	
exciting		popular	
expensive		selfish	

C. (irregular)

good	better	bad	worse

20 Past simple

A. (regular)

+ ed		walk		live	
cook	_cooked_	want		love	
jump		watch		graduate	
play		work		practice	
start		+ d		y + ied	
stay		hate	_hated_	study	_studied_
visit		like		try	

B. (irregular)

be	was/were	get		sell	
bring	brought	give		send	
buy	bought	go		shut	
catch	caught	have		sing	
come	came	hit		sit	
cut	cut	know		sleep	
do	did	leave		speak	
drink	drank	lose		stand	
drive		make		take	
eat		meet		teach	
fight		put		think	
find		read		wear	
fly		ride		win	
forget		see		write	

C. (went + -ing)

bowl	_bowled_	_went bowling_	shop		
camp			run	_ran_	
climb			swim	_swam_	
fish			cycle		
ski			dive		
surf			hike		
jog			skate		

Answers 20B (irregular verbs): drive-drove, eat-ate, fight-fought, find-found, fly-flew, forget-forgot, get-got, give-gave, go-went, have-had, hit-hit, know-knew, leave-left, lose-lost, make-made, meet-met, put-put, read-read, ride-rode, see-saw, sell-sold, send-sent, shut-shut, sing-sang, sit-sat, sleep-slept, speak-spoke, stand-stood, take-took, teach-taught, think-thought, wear-wore, win-won, write-wrote.

A Guide to the Communication Activities

Use these instructions with the Communication Activities on the third page of each unit.

☞ The photocopiable material needed for every "C" activity can be found in the Teacher's Book.

1A Crossword

The students write words which say something about themselves - e.g. their first name, their family name, their nationality, the city they live in. They fit the words together to make a crossword.

1B Newspaper reporters

In pairs, the students try to find out as much as they can about each other. They then tell the whole class what they have found out.

1C Around the World

☞ Use the *Around the World* board game to practice sentences like *She's from China*, *He lives in Rome*. The rules and board for this game are in the Teacher's Book.

2A Starting letter

One student says whether he/she is thinking of a city, a mountain etc. and says the starting letter. The other students take turns to ask Yes/No questions to try and find out what he/she is thinking of, using the structures they have learned - e.g. *Is it large? Is it in Africa?* If the answer is *Yes*, the student can guess the name of the place. If the answer is *No*, the turn passes to the next student.

2B Chase the ace

Remove three aces from a deck of cards and deal out the rest. Make a list of the cards, and write an adjective next to each number. In turn, each student takes a card from the student on the left. Whenever somebody makes a pair, he/she places it on the table and says a sentence which includes the corresponding adjective. The aim is to avoid having the ace at the end of the game.

2C Opinion poll

☞ In pairs, the students ask each other the questions in the photocopied lists. They then report their answers to the class and analyze the results - if these are presented as fractions or percentages, help the students do the calculation in English.

3A Where are they in your house?

One student asks another where things are in his/her house. The second student describes the exact location.

3B Neighborhoods

One student draws a grid of the streets in his/her neighborhood and gives it to the other student. The first student describes his/her neighborhood, and the second student tries to draw what he/she says on the grid.

3C Hiding in a picture

☞ Place one of the pictures so that all the students can see it. One student imagines he/she is in the picture, and the others guess where he/she is.

4A Directions

Students imagine they are at point A, B, C, or D. One student asks another how to get to places on the map. The student giving directions can then ask the other student to do something at each destination. The student not giving directions should pretend they don't understand and ask a lot of questions.

4B Bulls-eye

Divide the class into two or more teams, and give one student from each team a piece of chalk or board marker, and a blindfold to put on. Draw a simple target on the board for each team. The idea is for the blindfolded students to touch the target with their chalk/marker. They get more points for hitting the target nearer the center. Each team directs their masked team member to the target by calling out instructions. The game works well as a relay.

4C Maps of New York and London

☞ Use the maps in the Teacher's Book or other maps which you think your students will find interesting. Each student places a counter on the map to indicate where they are. They then pretend to telephone each other and describe where they are. One suggests a meeting place and tells the other how to get there. They then choose other locations.

5A Discovering a picture

One student secretly draws (or looks at) a picture, and writes down a list of between five and ten main things which are in it. They then write the same number of things which are not in it (the number should be decided in advance). Next, they show this list to a second student. The second student has half as many guesses as things in the list and must use the pattern *Are there any ...?* If the answer is *Yes, there are two/Yes, there's one* the student asks *Where is it/are they?* and tries to draw part of the picture on another piece of paper. They get one point for a correct guess and another one for drawing it in the correct location.

5B Where am I from?

One student imagines he/she is from a different country. The other students take turns to ask Yes/No questions to try and find out what the country is, using the patterns *Are there ...?* or *Is there ...?* After a student asks a question, he/she throws a dice. A 4 or 5 means he/she can have one guess, and a 6 means he/she can have three

A Guide to the Communication Activities

guesses. 1, 2, and 3 means the turn passes to the next student.

5C   What are the differences?
In pairs, the students ask questions alternately, trying to find the differences between two similar pictures. They do this by asking *Is there ...?* and *Are there ...?* questions. When a student answers *Yes ...*, he/she also gives the location.

6A   Go Fish!
If the class is large, divide it into groups and give each group a deck of cards (use either special *Go Fish* cards or normal playing cards). Deal out about half the deck, and place the rest in a pile in the middle. In turn, the students try to collect sets of four by asking other students for cards, saying *Do you have any ...?* If the answer is *Yes*, he/she receives the card(s) and has another turn. If the answer is *No. Go Fish!* he/she has to take the top card from the pile. A student must ask for a number which he/she has at least one of.

6B   Vampire grid game
Each student draws two 6 x 6 grids on a piece of paper, numbering them 1-6 horizontally and lettering them A-F vertically. The board illustration shows the number and shape of squares which each family member should occupy. Each student secretly chooses their location and draws or blocks out the appropriate squares on one of their grids. In pairs, students try to guess the location of each other's Dracula family members using the pattern *Do you have anything in (B5)?* If an answer is *Yes*, the student can ask another *Do you have ...* question.

6C   Shopping role-play
Some of the class are store owners and are dealt out cards which say what their stores sell. The other students are dealt shopping lists and money, and go to each store in turn, trying to buy what is on their lists.

7A   What's on the tray?
Place small objects or flash cards on a tray, and cover them with a cloth. Remove the cloth for a short time. The students try to remember what is on the tray. Replace the cloth. The students say or write sentences about each object/flash card they can remember.

7B   Prompts
One student names something countable or uncountable (e.g. *truck, eraser, yogurt*). The other(s) has to describe where the thing is (e.g. *There's a truck in the parking lot near this school*). This must be done within a short time limit. This can be made into a game with points.

7C   Menus
The simple version is for the students to order meals using the photocopied menus. Alternatively, get the students to go through the whole process of telephoning to make a reservation, arriving at the restaurant, sitting down, being served, paying, and leaving the restaurant.

8A   Guess who
One person makes a series of statements and questions about a well-known person/group (either to the whole class in teams, to a group, or in pairs). To practice the pronoun *his*, say things like *His hair's brown. Who is he?* or *His songs are popular. Who is he?* To practice the pronoun *her*, say things like *Her car's red. Who is she?* or *Her team's very strong. Who is she?* To practice *their*, say things like *Their uniform is red and white. Who are they?* or *Their drummer has long hair. Who are they?* Each student (team) has ten seconds to make a guess, and if they can't say anything within the time limit, allow anybody from any team to

try. Teams get one point for guessing correctly. Follow up by doing the activity in pairs or small groups.

8B   Bleep
One person makes a series of statements and questions. To practice *Our...*, say things like *Our bleeps are long. What are they? Our bleeps are noisy at night. What are they?* (instead of the bleeps, use any other sound or word, as long as it is always the same). To practice possessives (-'s), say things like *Akiko's bleep is black. What is it?* or *Akiko's bleep has four legs. What is it?* If the class is in teams, a team which guesses correctly after the first sentence gets 10 points, after the second 7, after the third 4, after the fourth 2, and after the fifth 1.

8C   Whose is it?
Each student has a photocopied page of a collection of objects. One asks the other who he/she thinks each object belongs to, and writes his/her guesses down. One student, or the teacher, has a master sheet with his/her guesses on it. Each student gets one point for a guess which is the same as on the master sheet. If the students like drawing, the activity can be extended by using pictures which they have drawn.

9A   Telepathy
Write some actions on the board or show the students some flash cards. One student secretly chooses one of the actions, closes his/her eyes, concentrates on the sentence (e.g. *He's watching a video*), and tries to transmit it to the other student(s). The other student(s) close their eyes, try to guess the sentence, and then compare their guesses to see who is telepathic (and maybe get points). This activity can be done in pairs, groups or as a whole class. Gradually make the actions more difficult.

A Guide to the Communication Activities

9B   Name a time

One student says a time, and the other student(s) imagines what each member of his/her family and friends are doing at that time.

9C   Detectives

Use the *Detectives* board game to practice sentences like *I think the President is taking a shower in the garden.* The rules and board for this game are in the Teacher's Book.

10A   Fashion parade

One student models in front of the class, another student announces. The student who has just modelled becomes the announcer for the next student.

10B   Guess who

Copy the boardwork from the picture. One student thinks of a well-known person, and describes him/her one sentence at a time, using the patterns on the board. Each student (or team, if the class is large) has one guess or a guess after each sentence. A student who guesses correctly after the first sentence gets 10 points, after the second sentence 7 points etc.

10C   What are the differences?

The students try to find ten differences between ten similar pictures. They do this by taking turns to describe what each of the people in the picture is wearing.

11A   Newspaper reporters

In pairs, the students try to find out as much as they can about what each other can do. They then tell the whole class what they have found out.

11B   I can see ...

One student thinks of something he/she can see in the room, through the window, in a picture, or something he/she can imagine seeing in another place (the beach, the park, etc.) and says the first letter. The others guess what it is.

11C   Survivors

A ship is sinking and there are only two life jackets. Each student has a role-play card, and makes *I can ...* sentences to justify why he/she should have a life jacket. The students vote to decide who gets the life jackets – they can't vote for themselves. Instead of using role-play cards, the students can choose which famous person they want to be. If the class is large, divide it into teams. Each team has to think of ten *I can ...* sentences, and only one team gets a life jacket.

12A   What's my job?

One student imagines he/she has a different occupation. The others take turns to ask Yes/No questions to try and discover the occupation. If an answer is *Yes*, the student who asked the question tries to guess the occupation. If the answer is *No*, the turn passes to the next student.

12B   Last sentence

One student (or you) writes an occupation on the board. The students take turns to make sentences about the occupation. The last student (or team) to make a sentence is the winner.

12C   Concentration

All the cards are put face down on a table. The students take turns to turn over two cards. If an occupation and description match, the student takes the pair and has another turn. If not, the turn passes to the next student.

13A   Twenty questions

One student imagines he/she has a different occupation. The others take turns to ask up to 20 Yes/No questions to try and find out what the occupation is. The answers (except to guesses) have to be qualified by an adverb of frequency. A student who guesses correctly with the first question gets 20 points, with the second question 19 points, etc. If nobody guesses within 20 questions, the student who is answering gets 20 points.

13B   Famous people

One student thinks of a famous person. Teams take turns to make sentences about the person – each sentence must include an adverb of frequency. The last team to make a sentence is the winner.

13C   Housework

Each student has a table which is half-filled with information about how much housework is done by some of the characters in the story. They exchange information by asking and answering questions. Then the students exchange the same information about each other.

14A   Lifestyles

The students look at pictures of people and imagine their lifestyles. Encourage the students to say whatever they want.

14B   Where is it?

One student secretly thinks of either a place in the city or another city. He/she says where the starting place is (a bus stop or station), and makes sentences one by one, using the patterns on the board. The other students try to guess the destination. Each person or team has only one guess or can guess after each sentence. A correct guess after the first sentence is worth 10 points, after the second 7 points, after the third 4 points, and after the fourth 2 points.

14C   Schedules

Each student has a schedule with information which is half-filled in, and some questions which need answering.

A Guide to the Communication Activities

15A Lifestyles
The students look at pictures of people and try and imagine their lifestyles. They make sentences which include adverbs of frequency.

15B How often?
Divide the class into teams. One student chooses something which people commonly do. Each student secretly writes down how often he/she does that thing. Each member of one team guesses the answer of each of the opposing team (in large classes, students make guesses about one member of the other team). A team gets one point for each correct answer. To make the game fair, restrict the choices of answers.

15C Questionnaire
In pairs, the students ask each other the questions in the questionnaire. The questions review the first fifteen units.

16A Team advice
Divide the class into two teams. A student from one team thinks of a problem. Each of the students from the other team quickly gives advice, one after the other, without pausing. They can't repeat any advice given by either team. They get a point for each piece of advice.

16B Good advice?
Divide the class into two teams. A student from one team secretly writes down a problem. Each member of the opposing team gives advice. The student who thought of the problem then reveals the problem. The team giving advice gets one point for every bit of advice which is appropriate.

16C Mime
Divide the class into teams. Place the problem cards in a pile the same distance from each of the teams. A student from each team turns over a card, hurries to his/her team, and

mimes the problem. After the team has guessed the problem, they give some advice, and another member of the team hurries to look at the next card. The winning team is either the one which guesses the most number of times within a time limit, or the one which does this a certain number of times.

17A Superstar
Divide the class into two teams. One team chooses which "superstar" they are. A student from the other team asks a student from the "superstar" team *What are you doing (at 6:00 on Wednesday afternoon, next week, etc.)?* The answer has to be given without hesitation, and previous answers can't be repeated. If a whole team (or a certain number of students) answers questions successfully, they get a point. If a student can't answer, the next team tries, and plays for two points. The points which teams play for escalate until one team scores. The game should be played at a fast pace.

17B No pausing
In pairs, Student A invites Student B to do something at a certain time. B refuses with a reason, and invites A to do something else at a different time. This continues until one student hesitates or repeats something.

17C Find your partners
Each student has an appointment calendar of the following week. They move around the class trying to find out who they are meeting each evening, asking questions like *What are you doing (on Saturday evening)?*

18A Which country is it?
One student thinks of a country, and says things you can do there. After each sentence, the other students try and guess what the country is. Each student (or each team, if the class is large) either has only one guess or a guess after each sentence.

18B How many questions?
One student says where he/she would like to go. The other students ask suitable follow-up questions in turn, and without hesitating or repeating a question. The one who asks the most questions is the winner.

18C World Cup
Use the *World Cup* board game to practice sentences like *I go swimming once a week*. The rules and board for this game are in the Teacher's Book.

19A Guess who
One student thinks of a person the students know, and describes him/her one sentence at a time, using a different adverb each time. The student answering (or team, if the class is large) has only one guess or can make a guess after each sentence. A student who guesses correctly after the first sentence gets 10 points, after the second 7 points, after the third 4 points, after the fourth 2 points, and after the fifth 1 point. The maximum number of sentences is five.

19B Leaving the room
One student leaves the room. The others choose an adverb. The student who left the room comes back and mimes actions to illustrate various adverbs until he/she has correctly mimed the chosen adverb. The class say things like *No! Not romantically!*

19C Mime
Divide the class into two teams, and put two piles of cards face down on a table which is the same distance from each team. One pile of cards is for actions and the other is for adverbs. One student from each team turns over a card from each pile, hurries back to his/her team, and mimes what was on the cards. When a team has guessed the action and adverb, another student hurries to look at another pair of cards. The winning

A Guide to the Communication Activities

team is either the one to make the most correct guesses within a time limit, or the one to first make a certain number of correct guesses.

20A Sentences

Write *All, Most, Some, One, None* on the board. Divide the class into teams. One student from one team makes a sentence starting with *All ...*, a student from the other (next) team makes a sentence starting with *Most ...* etc. They go through the list a number of times. Sentences can't be repeated.

20B Pairs

Divide the class into teams. A student from one team writes two words on the board and challenges a member of the other team to make sentences connecting them. The sentences must begin with *Both, One, or Neither*. If he/she succeeds, the team gets a point. If not, the challenger's team gets a point.

20C Dominoes

Share out most of the pieces, place one face up to start the game, and place the others face down. The students take turns to add a piece to either end of the chain on the table. When doing so, they must justify the connection saying *Both ...* If a student can't place a piece, he/she picks up one which is face down. The first student to get rid of all his/her pieces is the winner.

21A Routines

In pairs, one student goes through his/her daily routine in sequence. If he/she pauses, the other student asks questions to keep the conversation going.

21B Miming sequences

One student mimes a series of actions which illustrate how to do something (e.g. play tennis, rob a bank, repair something, do a trick, brush your teeth). The other student(s) tries to guess what the sequence of mimes demonstrates.

21C How do you ...?

One student draws or is dealt a card telling him/her what to ask the other student (e.g. *How do you boil an egg?*). They then ask the other student for more precise instructions and question anything which is not clear.

22A Consequences

Copy the boardwork from the picture. Give each of the students a piece of paper to fold into eight. Each student writes an answer to the first question on the first part, folds the piece of paper so the answer is hidden, and passes the paper to the next student. They then write the answer to the second question and pass it on, etc. After all the questions have been answered, the students unfold the pieces of paper they are holding, and read out what is written.

22B Crystal ball

Write a list of future dates and days on the board. In pairs, the students make predictions about what is going to happen on those dates and days (a crystal ball makes the activity more fun!). Keep a record of what they predict, and see which predictions are accurate.

22C Palmistry

Photocopy the palmistry guide and give it to each of the students. They use it to tell each other's fortune.

23A Newspaper reporters

In pairs, the students try to find out as much as they can about what each other has to do. They then tell the whole class what they have found out.

23B What's my job?

One student imagines he/she has a different occupation. In order to find out what the occupation is, the others ask Yes/No questions, which include "have to". After a student asks a question, he/she throws a dice. A 4 or

5 means he/she can have one guess, and a 6 means he/she can have three guesses.

23C Grand Prix

Arrange copies of the prompt cards (make more than one copy of each card). The students throw a dice and race around the track, making "have to" sentences for the cards they land on. Before starting, decide the number of laps required to complete the race.

24A Pictures of people

The students look at pictures of people, describe them, and imagine what their characters are like.

24B Criminals

Divide the class into two teams (or pairs if the class is large). A student from one team quickly flashes a picture of a person. The other team has to describe the picture, getting a point for each correct detail.

24C The Zodiac

Give the students copies of the Zodiac character chart. The students compare these character descriptions to themselves and the people they know.

25A Where am I?

A student imagines he/she is in a different place. The others ask Yes/No questions to try and find out what the place is. If an answer is *Yes*, the student who asked the question asks another question using the pattern *What ... like?* and can then make a guess. If an answer is *No*, the turn passes to the next student.

25B A place you know well

One student describes a place he/she knows well. The other student(s) ask for more details, trying to get as much information as possible.

A Guide to the Communication Activities

25C World strategies game

☞ In pairs students play the World strategies game to practice patterns using "like" (e.g. *What's Seoul like? It's ...*). The rules and board for this game are in the Teacher's Book.

26A Put them in order

Either you or one of the students write a list of animals, objects, or people on the board. Each student puts them in an order which they then justify, using comparative sentences.

26B Sevens

Make a list of cards from 2 to ace and write an adjective next to each number. Deal out about half a deck of cards and place the rest face down in a pile (if the class is large, divide it into groups and give each group a deck). One student places a 7 on the table. The next student either places another 7 or a 6/8 of the same suit as the first 7. The following students place cards which fit next to existing cards, until one student has no cards left. A student who can't place a card, picks one up. Every time a student places a card, he/she makes a comparative sentence which includes the corresponding adjective.

26C Twenty questions

☞ Arrange the prompt cards in a circle. A student throws a dice and moves a counter around the circle. If he/she lands on double or triple points he/she throws again. The other cards indicate whether he/she should think of an animal, country, etc. When this has been determined, the other students take turns to ask Yes/No questions which include a comparative (e.g. *Is it larger than Paris?*), or they can make a guess (e.g. *Is it Mexico City?*). A student who guesses correctly with the first question gets 20 points, with the second 19 points, etc. If nobody guesses correctly, the student who is answering gets 20 points. These points may be doubled, tripled or more.

27A Boasting

One student makes a boast about something which is related to him/her in some way. The next student makes a boast comparing something which relates to him/her with the thing which relates to the first student.

27B What is it?

In pairs, one student thinks of something in the room (or in a picture). To find out what it is, the other should ask Yes/No questions, which include a comparative. He/she can make a guess every five questions.

27C Comparing countries

☞ Use the *Around the World* board game to practice sentences like *Japan has a higher GNP than France*. The rules and board for this game are in the Teacher's Book.

28A Photographs and pictures

The students look at photographs of people. If the person is alive, the students describe their life. If they are no longer alive, the students describe their past. What the students say can be true or imaginary.

28B Who was I?

One student thinks of a person from the past. The other students take turns to ask Yes/No questions to try and find out who it is. If an answer is *Yes*, the student can make a guess. If an answer is *No*, the turn passes to the next student.

28C Last sentence

☞ Divide the class into two teams. A student from one team picks up a prompt card, shows it to all, and makes a sentence about the person on the card. A student from the other team then makes another sentence. The teams alternate, and the last team to make a sentence is the winner.

29A Where was my vacation?

In pairs, one student thinks of a place he/she went to on vacation (real or imaginary). The other asks Yes/No questions to find out where the vacation was. He/she can make a guess after every five questions.

29B Chain story

One student starts a story with (*A person the students know) went to ...* the other students take turns to add sentences to the story. If a student repeats a verb, he/she (or the team) is out.

29C Picture story

☞ The students tell stories from pictures. There are two picture strips in the Teacher's Book, but almost any comic strip can be used. (It is usually best to remove the words and let the students use their imagination. Another way is to leave the dialogue in the comic strip and have the students put it into the past tense.)

30A Name a time

Copy the boardwork from the picture. In pairs, one student says a time in the past and challenges the other to make a sentence with each of the board prompts.

30B True/False

One student makes a sentence about his/her past, and the other students guess whether it is true or false. This can be played as a class (all those who are wrong are out) or in teams (the opposing team gets one point for each correct guess).

30C Questionnaire

☞ In pairs, the students ask each other the questions in the questionnaire. The questions review all thirty units.

Author's acknowledgement for the activities

None of the activities in this book have been consciously copied from other sources, but many of the ideas have almost certainly been stimulated by ideas in other books which include learner-centered activities or by discussions with teachers who have read these books. It is impossible to know who had the original idea which led to each of the activities included in this course, so in appreciation of the hard work and imaginative ideas of all authors and teachers in this field, I am including a suggested reading list. All of the following materials contain ideas for language activities and games, and deserve a place on the bookshelf of all EFL/ESL teachers.

Action Plans. Macdonald, M., Rogers-Gordon, S. (Newbury House)

Alternatives. Baudains, R. and M. (Longman)

Back & Forth. Palmer, A., Rodgers, T., Olsen, J. (Prentice Hall) *Bridge The Gap.* Ferrer, J., Werner, P. (Prentice Hall)

Caring and Sharing in the Foreign Language Class. Moskowitz, G. (Newbury House)

Communication Games - Elementary, Intermediate and Advanced. Hadfield, J. (Nelson)

Communication Starters. Olsen, J. (Pergamon)

Communicative Ideas. Norman, D., Levihn, U., Hedenquist, J. (LTP)

Creative Grammar Practice. Gerngross, G., Puchta, H. (Longman)

English Puzzles - 1, 2, 3 and *4.* Case, D. (Heinemann)

ESL Teacher's Activities Kit. Claire, E. (Prentice Hall)

Favorite Games for All EFL-ESL Classes. Woodruff-Wieding, M., Ayala, L. (Sky Oaks).

Five Minute Activities. Ur, P., Wright, A. (CUP).

Games for All Reasons. Schultz, M., Fisher, A. (Addison-Wesley)

Games for Language Learning. Wright, A., Betteridge, D., Buckby, M. (CUP)

Games Language People Play. Steinberg, J. (Dominie)

Grammar in Action. Frank, C., Rinvolucri, M. (Prentice Hall)

Grammar Games. Rinvolucri, M. (CUP)

Grammar Practice Activities. Ur, P. (CUP)

Headstarts. Hess, N. (Longman)

How to Use Games in Language Teaching. Rixon, S. (Macmillan).

Keep Talking. Klippel, F. (CUP)

Language Teaching Games and Contests. Lee, W. (OUP).

Learner-Based Teaching. Campbell, C., Kryszewska, H. (OUP)

Lessons from the Learner. Deller, S. (Longman)

Play Games With English - 1, 2 and *3.* Granger, C. (Heinemann)

Recipes for Tired Teachers (2 books). Sion, C. (ed) (Addison-Wesley)

Take 5. Carrier, M. (Nelson)

Tandem Plus. Read, C., Matthews, A. (Nelson)

The Card Book. Abigail, T., McKay, H. (Prentice Hall)

The Recipe Book. Lindstromberg, S. (ed) (Longman)

Timesavers for English Teachers (Mary Glasgow)

Tombola. Palim, J., Power, P., Vannuffel, P. (Nelson)

Vocabulary. Morgan, J., Rinvolucri, M. (OUP)

Word Games With English -1, 2, 3 and *Plus.* Howard-Williams, D., Herd, C. (Heinemann)

Practical English Teaching magazines (Mary Glasgow)